Teaching Handbook Reception/P1

Linda Tallent

OXFORD
UNIVERSITY PRESS

Project X *Alien Adventures* Team

Series Consultants: Jennifer Chew, Maureen Lewis, Janice Pimm, Linda Tallent

Scottish Curriculum consultant: Gill Friel
Welsh Curriculum consultant: Pat Griffiths
Northern Ireland Curriculum consultant: Rachel Russ
Inside cover notes and PCMs: Christine Cork, Linda Tallent
Illustrations by: Jonatronix Ltd.

Project X concept by Rod Theodorou and Emma Lynch

The publisher wishes to thank the following schools for their valuable contribution to the trialling and development of **Project X *Alien Adventures*:** Birtley East Community Primary School, County Durham; Eastry Church of England Primary School, Sandwich; Featherby Infant and Nursery School, Gillingham; Goldington Green Lower School, Bedford; Halebank CE (VC) Primary School, Widnes; Kirkby Church of England Primary School, Kirkby; Lakeside Primary School, Camberley; Larkrise Primary School, Oxford; Littleton Green Primary School, Cannock; Newsham Primary School, Blyth; Walton Oak Primary School, Walton-on-Thames; Wickhambreaux CE Primary School, Canterbury.

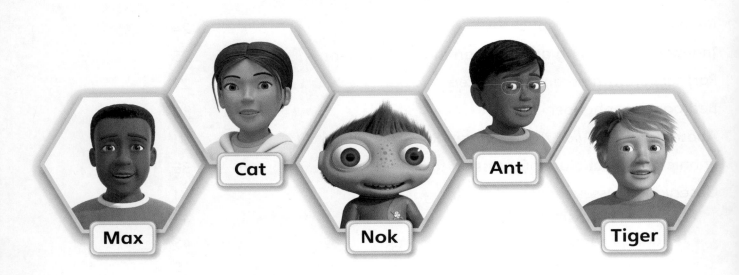

OXFORD
UNIVERSITY PRESS

Great Clarendon Street, Oxford, OX2 6DP,
United Kingdom

Oxford University Press is a department of the University of Oxford.
It furthers the University's objective of excellence in research, scholarship,
and education by publishing worldwide. Oxford is a registered trade mark of
Oxford University Press in the UK and in certain other countries

© Oxford University Press 2013
First Edition published in 2013

All rights reserved. No part of this publication may be reproduced, stored in a retrieval
system, or transmitted, in any form or by any means, without the prior permission in writing
of Oxford University Press, or as expressly permitted by law, by licence or under terms
agreed with the appropriate reprographics rights organization. Enquiries concerning
reproduction outside the scope of the above should be sent to the Rights Department,
Oxford University Press, at the address above.

You must not circulate this work in any other form
and you must impose this same condition on any acquirer
British Library Cataloguing in Publication Data
Data available
978-0-19-849287-0

3 5 7 9 10 8 6 4 2

Paper used in the production of this book is a natural, recyclable product
made from wood grown in sustainable forests. The manufacturing process conforms
to the environmental regulations of the country of origin.
Printed in Great Britain by Bell and Bain Ltd

Acknowledgements
Illustrations by Jonatronix Ltd
Project X concept by Rod Theodorou and Emma Lynch
The publisher would like to thank the following for permission to reproduce photographs:
p27 OUP/photodisk. All other images © Oxford University Press.

Contents

Welcome to Project X	4
Blast off with Project X *Alien Adventures*!	6
Project X *Alien Adventures* structure chart	8
Getting the most out of Project X *Alien Adventures*	10
Giving boys a reason to read	14
The importance of developing independent readers	17
The process of reading	19
The importance of talk, reading aloud and reading partners	21
Reading partner prompt sheet	24
Independent reading and the learning environment	25
Partnership with parents and carers	27
Bedroom door hanger	30
About Project X *Alien Adventures* in Reception/P1	31
Phonic and vocabulary progression for Reception/P1	36
Observation, assessment and planning	41
• Reading assessment records	43
• Phonic progression assessment records	45
• Comprehension assessment record	48
• Children's 'I can' statements	49
Reading and writing certificates	59
Project X *Alien Adventures* and the Scottish Curriculum for Excellence	61
Project X *Alien Adventures* and the Foundation Phase in Wales	65
Project X *Alien Adventures* and the Northern Ireland Curriculum	68
Photocopiable Masters	72

Welcome to Project X

Project X is the overarching name for a series of highly engaging and effective reading programmes published by Oxford University Press. As well as the brand new **Project X** *Alien Adventures* programme for independent reading, the series includes a comprehensive, whole-school guided reading programme (the original 'Project X' – Project X ORIGINS), a small, focused phonics programme (Project X PHONICS), and a reading intervention programme (Project X CODE). Drawing on research evidence, classroom practice and a real understanding of what makes modern children tick, it has everything you need to make learning both effective and fun.

The materials that make up **Project X** have been developed with the very best educational experts.

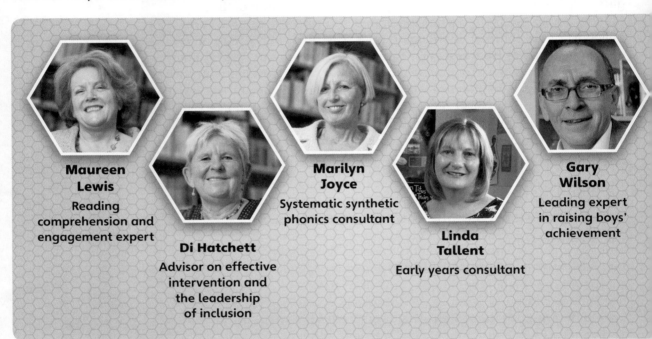

Maureen Lewis – Reading comprehension and engagement expert

Di Hatchett – Advisor on effective intervention and the leadership of inclusion

Marilyn Joyce – Systematic synthetic phonics consultant

Linda Tallent – Early years consultant

Gary Wilson – Leading expert in raising boys' achievement

What makes Project X unique?

All of the programmes within Project X share the same aim: to motivate and raise the achievement of 21st century children, especially boys.

This doesn't mean that **Project X** isn't for girls – far from it. What it does mean is that, unlike any other reading programme, **Project X** provides teaching and learning resources explicitly designed to support boys, whilst not disadvantaging girls.

The gender gap in achievement in reading and writing is something many schools still need to address, with white, working-class boys at the greatest disadvantage.

According to the Ofsted framework schools will be judged on how they respond to the needs of particular groups of pupils by observing how well they make progress and fulfill their potential. Boys' achievement comes under this guideline. It is imperative, therefore, to try and help to close the gender gap.

Engaging group reading with a phonics focus

Reception/P1–Year 1/P2
40 fiction and non-fiction books

A guided-reading programme that engages all children

Reception/P1–Year 6/P7
Over 200 books

Blast off on an incredible independent reading journey!

Reception/P1–Year 4/P5
96 books

A breakthrough for SEN and struggling readers

Provides rapid catch-up for children from Year 2 onwards. 56 books

There is a wealth of research evidence to show that boys, far more than girls, require specific strategies to engage them with learning. 'Boy-friendly books' are a big part of the appeal of **Project X**, but they are only part of the solution to engaging boys. The series also draws on a wealth of evidence from research, case studies and various Raising Boys' Achievement initiatives to provide teachers with strategies and approaches that are proven to be effective with boys. What's more, having engaged boys in the classroom gives teachers more time to ensure that every child is being helped to progress at the right pace. And some girls can really benefit from the lively, imaginative conversations that engaged boys participate in.

The other unique feature of **Project X** is the original, exciting character adventure that sits at the heart of the series from Reception/P1 right through to Year 6/P7. Readers can follow the varied adventures of Max, Cat, Ant and Tiger – four ordinary children with extraordinary watches that allow them to shrink to micro-size. Research shows that familiar characters are the number 1 hook for young readers, particularly boys, and because the characters evolve and have different adventures **Project X** offers both familiarity and variety. As well as engaging children with reading, these characters and stories provide children with a wealth of stimulus for talk and writing … and even playground play! The characters also give children common ground – whatever their age, ability or level of achievement, every child could be reading a **Project X** book, talking about the characters and sharing their experiences with their friends.

Look out for: *Big Writing Adventures* … coming in early 2014

Oxford University Press has been working with Ros Wilson to develop an exciting new writing programme for Years 2–6/Primary 3–7. *Big Writing Adventures* combines the powerful **Big Writing** methodology with a series of highly engaging 'writing missions', some of which involve the Project X characters. For schools in England, the programme also provides valuable clarity of progression through the new English curriculum.

Visit **www.oxfordprimary.co.uk** to find out more.

Blast off with Project X *Alien Adventures!*

Join Max, Cat, Ant and Tiger as they embark on an exciting new independent reading journey!

Project X *Alien Adventures* offers 96 amazing new stories, featuring Max, Cat, Ant and Tiger … and some new alien friends! Highly motivating, fully decodable, and with finer steps of progression than any other reading programme, these books are a great way to build children's confidence and enthusiasm and are ideal for independent reading.

The **Project X** *Alien Adventures* series fully supports the Statutory Framework for the Early Years Foundation Stage and the new National Curriculum. The curriculum stresses the importance of pupils having access to reading books that are consistent with their developing phonic knowledge and skills; the curriculum also states that: 'At the same time they will need to hear, share and discuss a wide range of high-quality books to develop a love of reading and broaden their vocabulary.'

Books they CAN read independently

The **Project X** *Alien Adventures* books are 100% decodable: the series follows a progressive systematic synthetic phonics structure, which correlates to *Letters and Sounds* Phases 1 to 6. In Reception/P1 and Year 1/P2, children have the chance to consolidate and practise the concepts and skills they have learned in their daily phonics sessions. The small steps of progression and fine levelling ensure that all children experience reading success right from the very beginning. In later books, Years 2–4 (P3–5), the careful levelling continues, building children's stamina, fluency and comprehension skills and ensuring that they develop as confident and 'hungry' readers.

Books they WANT to read and will love reading

Project X *Alien Adventures* is 100% fun. The series combines all the best ingredients of **Project X**: the stunning 3D artwork, the continuous plot and engaging stories, and the well-loved characters with some great new aliens, gadgets and vehicles.

FREE online resources!
Visit www.oxfordprimary.co.uk for lots of **Project X** *Alien Adventures* freebies, including: animations, bookmarks, door hangers and the new *Alien Adventures* game!

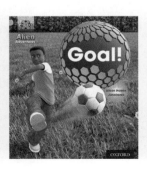

 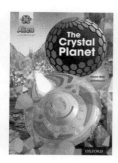 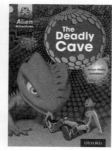 

The *Alien Adventures* story

Our adventures start when Nok, a micro-sized alien from Planet Exis, crash-lands on Earth. He soon meets four micro-sized children – Max, Cat, Ant and Tiger – who teach him about life on Earth. In later books our heroes find Nok's spaceship and blast off into space! So begins their series of action-packed, intergalactic adventures. Together, the micro-friends travel to Planet Exis, where they come up against a space villain called Badlaw and his army of robotic Krools. Our heroes then find out that they have to go on a mission to collect four fragments that form the Core of Exis in order to defeat Badlaw and save the galaxy! For more about the **Project X *Alien Adventures*** story in Reception/P1, see pages 31–35.

Project X *Alien Adventures* structure chart

Year	Oxford Level	Book Band		Letters and Sounds Phase	*Alien Adventures* books	*Alien Adventures* series companions	Teachers' Resources
Reception/Primary 1	1	Pre-Book Bands Lilac	A	Phase 1	• Max's Box • In the Sky		
			B	Phase 2, Set 1	• Splat! • Max's Rocket		
	1+	1 Pink	A	Phase 2, Set 2	• The Fishing Trip • Let's Bake!		
			B	Phase 2, Set 3	• Tin Cat • Sit, Cog Dog!		
			C	Phase 2, Set 4	• Get Ant! • Peg It Up		
			D	Phase 2, Set 5	• Run, Tin Cat! • Peck, Peck		
	2	2 Red	A	Phase 3, Set 6	• An Odd Bug • Nok Can Fix It		
			B	Phase 3, Set 7	• Cat's Picnic • A Bag of Tricks		
			C	Phase 3	• Moths! • Tiger's Fish		
	3	3 Yellow	A	Phase 3	• On Nok's Trail • I Win!		
			B	Phase 3	• Popcorn Surfing • Stuck in the Mud		
			C	Phase 3	• The Lost Cow • The Rocket Flight		
Year 1/Primary 2	4	4 Light Blue	A	Phase 4	• Cat's Painting • It's Too Hot!		
			B	Phase 4	• Helter-Skelter • Funfair Fun		
			C	Phase 4	• A Shock for Nok • Goal!		
	5	5 Green	A	Phase 5	• The Seagull • Claws		
			B	Phase 5	• The Parachute • Molly's New Toy		
			C	Phase 5	• Nok's Lunch • Nok Gets Homesick		
	6	6 Orange	A	Phase 5	• An Amazing Find • Blast Off!		
			B	Phase 5	• Don't Press the Buttons! • Worm Song		
			C	Phase 5	• Spacewalk • The Junk Cruncher		

Year	Oxford Level	Book Band	Letters and Sounds Phase	*Alien Adventures* books	*Alien Adventures* series companions	Teachers' Resources
Year 2/Primary 3	7	7 Turquoise	Phase 6	• Planet Exis • Attack of the Buzzles • The Empty Palace • Battle with the Beast • Nurp Stampede • The Trap		
	8	8 Purple	Phase 6	• Tiger x 4 • The Sands of Akwa • Holo-board Havoc • Ant's Pact • The Screams of the Raptiss • The Secret Whirlpool		
	9	9 Gold	Phase 6	• The Crystal Planet • The Ruby Cage • The Hunt for Nok • Race to the Pyramid • One Step Ahead • Chamber of Treasures		
	10	10 White	Phase 6	• Swamp Crash • Spaceship Graveyard • Fear Forest • Attack of the Giant Meeb • The Cave of Life • Save the World!		
	11	11 Lime		• Space Hunt • The Deadly Cave • Grumptus Attack • The Mines of Moxor • The Contest • Return to Exis		
Year 3/Primary 4	9	12 Brown		• The Destroyer • Space Rat Rescue • Crunch Time! • The Moon Winder		
	10			• Space Vultures • The Planet of Bones • Starmite Swarm • The Giants of Ariddas		
	11			• The Craggrox Awake • Attack of the Blobs • The Image Maker • Battle with Badlaw		
Year 4/Primary 5	12	13 Grey		• Badlaw's Revenge • The Rats of Rolia • Trapped in Time • Double Cross		
	13			• The Rust Monster • Pit-stop Peril • The Red Cutlass • Cyberbee Break Out		
	14			• Operation Holotanium • An Ancient Enemy • The Fury of Vogoss • The Waythroo Wormhole		

Primary/P references in this handbook relate to Primary year groups in Scotland and Northern Ireland.

Getting the most out of Project X *Alien Adventures*

The **Project X *Alien Adventures*** books are designed and levelled to support children's independent reading – either within school or at home – allowing them to practise and consolidate vital skills, build stamina and fluency, and develop that all-important love of reading right from day one. The series couldn't be easier to use.

Step 1: Get your children on board!

Animations are a great way to engage 21st century children, especially boys! Launch **Project X *Alien Adventures*** in your classroom with one of our short animations. These are a great stimulus for talk as they give a flavour of the adventures to come, much like a movie trailer, and can really help to generate a 'buzz' around the series. There are two animations, both of which are available free, online at www.oxfordprimary.co.uk.

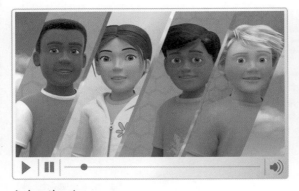

Animation 1

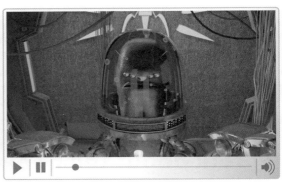

Animation 2

Step 2: Check out the *Alien Adventures* Companions

Accompanying the **Project X *Alien Adventures*** series are 3 companions designed to really hook children in and make them want to read the stories themselves. They give readers additional information about the special watches, the characters, the spaceship, spacesuits and gadgets, as well as comic strip adventures, jokes, games and things to make and do. They are perfect for generating talk … and perfect for wet breaktimes!

Step 3: Choose a reading book

The **Project X** *Alien Adventures* series is correlated to Book Bands, *Letters and Sounds* Phases (where appropriate) and the Oxford Levels so you and your pupils can organize, store and select books quickly and easily. The *Phonic progression assessment record* sheets will help you identify the band/level a child is comfortable reading at so that you can direct their book choice accordingly (see page 45–47 of this handbook).

On the back of each book from Lilac to White bands (Oxford Levels 1–10) you will find a brief summary of the phonic skills and high-frequency words covered. Should you wish to select a book to help a child practise a specific skill, you will find a full breakdown of the phonic and vocabulary progression at Reception/P1 on pages 36–40 of this handbook.

> ### Should I choose books for pupils or allow free choice?
>
> You know your children best and will often want to choose books that are at a level that is right for them. However, it is also important to give children a sense that they can freely choose their own books. These might be from the relevant Book Band/Oxford Level or from a wider library selection.
>
> If they sometimes want to just pick up a book and look at the pictures, or read a favourite 'easy' book, that's OK. The important thing is they are still getting a positive experience. Children need to choose any book they want in the classroom and *have a go* at it. They need to read fully-decodable books, familiar favourites and more challenging texts to develop fluency and a love of reading.

Step 4: Talk about the book

The importance of spoken language for developing pupils' vocabulary, grammar and their understanding for reading and writing is given high priority in the National Curriculum. On the inside front and back cover of every **Project X** *Alien Adventures* book, you will find notes which: give question prompts and points for discussion, highlight phonic practice words, point out the challenge words, and give additional activities that children can do. Children might do these activities with their peers, with an adult in school or with a parent/carer at home.

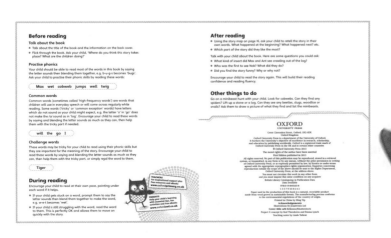

Step 5: Do a follow-up activity

For each book in the series there is a corresponding Photocopiable Master (PCM), which can be used for follow-up work to develop formative comprehension skills. There are also more generic PCMs for additional practice.

Step 6: Assessment

Support for assessing pupil progress against the requirements of the Early Years Foundation Stage, *Letters and Sounds* for phonics, and the National Curriculum (as appropriate) is provided in the Teaching Handbooks. See pages 41–60 for more information.

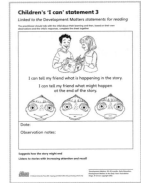

Free online resources

Visit: www.oxfordprimary.co.uk for other free *Alien Adventures* resources:
- bookmarks
- door hangers
- PCMs
- the **Project X** *Alien Adventures* game!

Professional development

For advice and top tips on developing early independent readers and working with parents as partners, watch the films by early years expert Linda Tallent free, online at: www.oxfordprimary.co.uk.

Supporting parents and carers

On the inside front and back cover of every book, you will find notes which: give question prompts and points for discussion, highlight phonic practice words, point out the challenge words, and give follow-up activities that parents and children can do together.

eBooks and online support

Oxford University Press' award-winning website for parents provides a wealth of support and advice to help families help children with their literacy and maths; it has a collection of **free eBooks**, including **Project X *Alien Adventures*** titles. Visit www.oxfordowl.co.uk to find out more.

For more advice on working with parents, see pages 16 and 27–30 of this handbook.

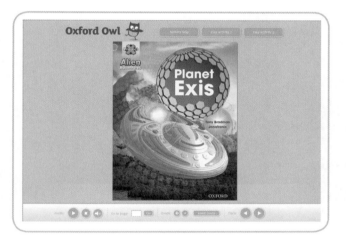

Giving boys a reason to read

Project X *Alien Adventures* has been created to meet the needs and interests of all children. However, there is a wealth of research showing that there are specific challenges involved in ensuring some boys become readers. Boys are more likely than girls to struggle with reading and to give up on independent reading. For these reasons **Project X** *Alien Adventures* has been designed to include content that will particularly motivate boys to read, while also appealing to girls.

Why do some boys struggle with reading?

The reasons for some boys' underperformance in literacy are complex and often include wider societal factors such as gender roles and stereotypes, family influences, behaviour issues, peer pressure and self-stereotyping. There are also factors relating directly to the teaching of reading such as boys' early reading experiences, teacher expectations, teaching and learning practices, learning contexts and book choice. One factor, however, stands out above all others when it comes to boys and learning, and that is *motivation*. When it comes to reading and writing boys, far more than girls, need to see a clear purpose for what they are doing. They won't simply do something because they are told to; they want to know what's in it for them. For some boys it's not that they can't, it's just that they can't be bothered!

Building identity

Readers can confirm and extend their own identity through reading and so build their confidence. The **Project X** characters think, act and feel in ways that modern children, particularly boys, will be able to relate to. However, they do not represent gender stereotypes. They show both active and affective aspects of identity. *Alien Adventures* also has a strong emphasis on teamwork. So, even though the stories themselves may be fantastical, readers can empathize with the characters and make links to their own lives.

Encouraging talk

Talking about and reflecting on books is a vital part of becoming a reader and talking to gather ideas is an important strategy for becoming a mark-maker/writer. Boys in particular benefit from articulating and reinforcing their thoughts and ideas through talk.

Communication and Language is a prime area in the Statutory Framework for the Early Years Foundation Stage. The new National Curriculum also stresses the importance of spoken language across the whole curriculum. The **Project X** *Alien Adventures* series can be used as a stimulus to support talk in a number of ways:

1. by watching the free online animations,
2. through use of the companion books,
3. through discussion around the exciting stories and on-going narrative,
4. through the in-book features, such as the *Retell the story* pages in Reception/P1–Year 1/P2,
5. by using the inside cover notes,
6. through follow-up activities.

ICT and multimedia

Today's children are growing up in a multimedia world. Research has shown that multimedia is an excellent way of engaging boys with literacy. As well as being highly engaging and motivating for children, films, cartoons, websites, computer games and other multimedia texts often present specific and sophisticated literacy challenges. It is important that pupils' experience in using such forms of literacy is acknowledged, appreciated and developed if they are to be fully literate in the 21st century.

Project X *Alien Adventures* responds to this in four ways.

1. The series aims to engage young readers by using a detailed, 3D digital illustration style in all the stories. This brings the world of films and computer games to books and has been a huge hit with children.
2. **Project X** *Alien Adventures* offers a number of eBooks that can be accessed online and used to engage children, stimulate discussion, and support both traditional and multimedia literacy skills.
3. The *Alien Adventures* animations can be used to introduce the series in a class session, which can help build anticipation and generate a 'buzz' around reading independently.
4. The *Alien Adventures* Companions encourage wider reading by providing additional information about the characters, gadgets and vehicles in a format that children will be familiar with from 'annuals' that accompany popular television series.

To access the FREE eBooks or watch the **Project X** *Alien Adventures* animations visit: **www.oxfordprimary.co.uk**

Purposeful learning and regular reviews of progress

Boys like to have a clear purpose in order to understand their reason for learning. They also like to see evidence of their progress as they find achievement and recognition motivating. **Project X Alien Adventures** takes the reader through small steps of progression and fine levelling as a way of ensuring boys experience success as readers from the very beginning.

Family involvement and reading role models

Parents/carers are important partners in helping children become readers and writers. It is important, for example, for boys to see others – particularly other males – reading. This reinforces the place that reading has in society and therefore the reasons for learning to read.

Teachers have a key role to play in working in partnership with parents to support their young children. Supporting families in building a reading culture at home is important so that boys see reading as something to engage with beyond the school setting/environment. Involving fathers or other males in reading with boys has been shown to be one successful way to encourage this. On the inside covers of each of the **Project X Alien Adventures** books there are some simple questions and activities to support parents/carers in reading with their children. For more information on working with parents, see pages 27–30.

Competitive approaches and celebrating achievement

Much of the research into raising boys' achievement shows that competitive approaches to learning can be effective. This doesn't mean setting children against each other but against their own personal targets. In each of the **Project X Alien Adventures** Teaching Handbooks, you will find a number of 'I can' statements to support pupils with monitoring their own success.

On-going praise, together with recognition and reward for success are vitally important to young learners, particularly boys. There are reading and writing certificate templates in each handbook that can be used to celebrate achievement.

FREE: Getting the Best out of Boys Kit

We've teamed up with Gary Wilson, one of the UK's leading experts on raising boys' achievement, to create a professional development kit for schools to help you get the best out of your boys. Visit **www.oxfordprimary.co.uk** to find out more.

The importance of developing independent readers

There is a huge body of evidence both nationally and internationally to suggest that reading independently, for pleasure, has a significant, positive effect on attainment.

- *Evidence suggests that there is a positive relationship between reading frequency, reading enjoyment and attainment.* (Clark 2011; Clark and Douglas, 2011).[1]
- *Regularly reading stories or novels outside of school is associated with higher scores in reading assessments.* (PIRLS, 2006; PISA, 2009).[2]
- *There is a positive link between positive attitudes towards reading and scoring well on reading assessments.* (Twist et al, 2007).[3]

Independent reading is the reading that we choose to do. It's the personal investment that we make in a book or a piece of writing. It can be about reading for a purpose or reading for pleasure: or it can be a combination of both.

Independent reading starts as soon as a child can hold a book and *should* happen long before they start school. If they can't decode the text at that point, it doesn't matter. It's about the experience of enjoying the stories and/or the information contained in a book; often, it's just about the child talking about the pictures. Of course, children will come to school with a whole range of experiences and many may not have had the same exposure to books as others in their class, so we need to ensure that all children have a positive experience of reading from the moment they step into the classroom.

[1/2/3] Education Standards Research Team, *Research evidence on reading for pleasure*, May 2012.

Young children also need to understand that reading is not just about 'learning and school' but that reading is about entertainment, enjoyment, finding stuff out, having tales to share with their friends, making their own choices ... and that sometimes they *won't* like reading something, but that's fine too! Giving children time and space to read independently – either on their own or in groups – allows them to develop their reading identity.

A child needs to believe they are 'a reader'. This perception of themselves is incredibly important – especially for boys – and it's a perception that will be formed very early on in their education.

One of the key aims for English in the National Curriculum is to ensure pupils 'develop the habit of reading widely and often, for both pleasure and information'. The more children read independently, the more confident they become in their ability to read. This confidence helps them to develop a positive relationship with books and a sense of ownership over them. If it's a fiction book, for example, they will look forward to reading about a character's development as they begin to share in the character's adventures and experiences.

If you have a good learning environment that fosters a love of books, if you read regularly to children and help guide their reading choices, and if the adult-led teaching is fun, multi-sensory, active and enjoyable, then ALL children cannot fail to get a positive reading experience, whatever their background.

Free professional development support

For more top tips on developing early independent readers, watch the Linda Tallent films free online at: **www.oxfordprimary.co.uk**

The process of reading

In order for children to become truly independent readers, they need to master the mechanics of reading. As their phonic knowledge progresses and their comprehension skills develop, so their confidence and enjoyment of reading will increase. When developing **Project X Alien Adventures** careful consideration was given to making sure that a gradual progression in phonics and comprehension was inherent in the stories, so children would be able to easily and confidently build their reading skills and experience success from the start.

The importance of systematic teaching of phonics

Systematic teaching of phonics is the key to children learning to read. This is confirmed by Ofsted's findings in their report 'Reading by six: how the best schools do it':

Concentrated and systematic use of phonics is key to their (children's) success; this is based on high-quality and expert teaching that gives pupils the opportunity to apply what they have learnt through reading, writing and comprehension of what they are reading.[1]

As stressed in the National Curriculum, understanding that letters on the page represent the sounds in spoken words underpins all reading. When children are learning to read, they need to be taught to use phonics as the *first strategy* for decoding unknown words. Children should not be prompted to use other cues such as saying the first sound and then guessing or looking at the illustration to see what word would 'fit'. Some words that occur frequently in texts are not completely phonically decodable. Children need to be taught these as common exception words (high-frequency, tricky words). When children encounter common exception words in their reading they should be encouraged to recognize the GPCs (Grapheme-Phoneme Correspondences) they contain as this will help them in their reading and spelling.

All **Project X** books fully support this approach, while also providing children with rich and engaging reading experiences. They are the perfect complement to any systematic synthetic phonics programme. Throughout Reception/P1 and Year 1/P2 the books have been carefully written to support children's emerging phonic knowledge and their ability to say letter sounds and blend sounds together in order to read new words. On pages 45–47 of this handbook, you will find *Phonic progression assessment records* to help you track pupils' progress.

Project X Phonics offers a lively, active approach to teaching phonics for Reception/P1 and Year 1/P2, combining all the best ingredients of **Project X** with a rigorous phonics structure. It offers a supportive bridge between phonics instruction and independent reading, allowing children to practise and consolidate the concepts and skills they learn in whole-class phonics teaching. Find out more about **Project X Phonics** at www.oxfordprimary.co.uk.

[1] Ofsted, *Reading by six: how the best schools do it*, © Crown copyright 2010.

Comprehension

One of the overarching aims for English in the National Curriculum is to ensure that pupils 'read easily, fluently and with good understanding'. Building children's comprehension skills is given a high priority in **Project X Alien Adventures**. Understanding what has been read is central to being an effective reader and to enjoying reading. Comprehension is not something that comes automatically. The latest research shows that children can be helped to develop comprehension skills by the explicit teaching of certain aspects of comprehension and by offering children specific strategies to help build these aspects. Over time children develop a repertoire of comprehension strategies that they can use across a range of texts.

The *Comprehension assessment record* on page 48 provides support in the assessment of comprehension skills of individual or groups of children.

Supporting children to develop as readers

In the early stages:

- Prompt children to use blending of phonemes as their main approach to decoding words.
- Teach children to recognize common words (high-frequency, decodable words) and common exception words (high-frequency, tricky words) by sight:
  - encourage them to look at the shape, length and any unique features of these words.
- Teach reading for meaning:
  - after a child has decoded the words in a sentence either reread the sentence to the child or prompt the child to reread the sentence themselves. This will encourage the child to activate their prior knowledge and further the child's understanding of what they have read.
- Teach children to use clues and illustrations around the text:
  - before reading, draw children's attention to the illustrations in the book and support them to predict what might happen in the text;
  - after reading, ask children factual questions and inferential questions about the text; this will support them to make meaning from the text.
- Positively encourage children to read independently:
  - ensure children have access to books that match their stage of phonic acquisition. Provide opportunities for children to talk to an adult or another child about what they have read.
  - provide a system for children to record the books they have read.

> ### Independent writing
>
> Reading and writing are mutually supportive skills, which is why those children who don't understand what it is to be a reader sometimes struggle to become writers. The carefully levelled **Project X Alien Adventures** books mean that children become confident readers from day one. The stories and the series companions can provide an exciting stimulus for children's own writing activities in class. In addition, there are PCMs to support each of the 96 books in the series; these can be used as a springboard for further writing activities (see pages 72–104 of this handbook).

The importance of talk, reading aloud and reading partners

Talk

One key factor in developing independent readers is all the talk that surrounds a book or a piece of writing. Children have a natural desire to share and pass on information that they have found out *themselves* with friends, teachers or family members. For young children this can give them the crucial confidence boost they need in order to develop independent thought, feeling and expression.

As we all know, many children do not have the opportunity at home to engage in conversation or to listen to stories being read to them on a regular basis and may have limited access to books. These children will not have had experience of internalising the rhythmic, repetitive pattern of story language and may have a limited vocabulary.

- *The number of picture books in the home has been positively linked to children's receptive and expressive language.*[1]
- *Familiarity with story books has been associated with young children's vocabulary and reading skills.*[2]
- *By the age of three, some children will already have heard over 33 million words said to them by their parents. Others will have heard only 10 million.*[3]

For these children, being given talking opportunities in the classroom is vital.

Tips: Try tuning in to talking opportunities. This is not planned talk, but all those opportunistic learning moments that we come across. It's about tuning in to what children are talking about, keeping that conversation going and encouraging a dialogue about books. For example, if you overhear a conversation about aliens, you could say things like, 'Do you know any films or TV shows about aliens? What do you remember about them? Have you read any books about aliens or spaceships?'

---

[1] Payne, A. C., Whitehurst, G. J., Angell, A. L., 'The role of home literacy environment in the development of language ability in preschool children from low-income families', *Early Childhood Research Quarterly* (1994), 9(3-4): 427–40.

[2] Senechal, M., LeFevre, J. A., Hudson, E., et al, 'Knowledge of storybooks as a predictor of young children's vocabulary', *Journal of Educational Psychology* (1996), 88(3): 520–36.

[3] Risley, T. R., and Hart, B., 'Promoting early language development', in Watt, N. F., Ayoub, C., Bradley, R. H., Puma, J. E., and LeBoeuf W. A. (Eds.), *The crisis in youth mental health: Critical issues and effective programs, Volume 4, Early intervention programs and policies*, (2006), 83–88.

The importance of reading aloud

If we want children to enjoy reading and to be motivated, independent readers, we need to demonstrate our own enthusiasm for reading. One of the best ways of doing this is to read aloud to them daily. Hearing stories read by adults has a strong impact on children's attitudes towards reading. It helps them develop a positive and long-lasting relationship with books.

> *A particular influence on young children's acquisition of language is the effect of shared book reading with adults. Findings show that early expressive language development was facilitated by joint reading strategies that engaged, supported and promoted children's active participation in the book reading opportunities. The longer a child stayed engaged in the book reading episode, and the more an adult encouraged the child's active participation by expanding on what a child says, or by asking open-ended questions, the greater the effect the reading experience had on the child's language development.*[1]

The National Curriculum programme of study (Year 1) states that pupils should be taught to develop pleasure in reading, motivation to read, and understanding by listening to and discussing stories at a level 'beyond which they can read independently'.

Modelling fluent expressive reading and encouraging children to respond to what they hear will develop their knowledge of stories, improve their listening skills and extend their vocabulary. Reading aloud enables you to:

- model what 'good reading' sounds like
- help children to develop the skill of mental imaging by reading dramatically and with expression
- nourish their imagination
- develop their listening skills
- provide them with an enjoyable experience.

Tips

Why not ask volunteers to come in and read? This could mean: dinner supervisors, parents, grandparents or older children within the school. This is not necessarily about reading *with* children, it could be reading *to* children. It's about reading role models and positive reinforcement of the reading experience. It's about having fun with books, rather than teaching reading. However, you may want to provide some support for your volunteers in case the children do want to read to them. For support for volunteers and parents, visit: **www.oxfordowl.co.uk**.

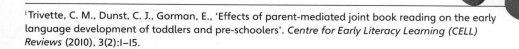

[1] Trivette, C. M., Dunst, C. J., Gorman, E., 'Effects of parent-mediated joint book reading on the early language development of toddlers and pre-schoolers'. *Centre for Early Literacy Learning (CELL) Reviews* (2010), 3(2):1–15.

Reading partners

Opportunities to read to and with a reading partner at a similar reading ability can encourage children to share their success as a reader and undertake joint problem-solving when they encounter difficulties. As the 'listener' has to follow the text as well, they too are practising their reading skills. Very early readers will enjoy 'play' reading to a partner, especially if this involves retelling a familiar book.

Reading partners should be encouraged to discuss the books they share: what they thought of them, what they learned and any questions they have. This will help build a culture in which children see reading as a social and pleasurable activity. You could also encourage reading partners to share some of their discussion with the rest of the class.

You will need to model reading partner practice and talk through the prompt sheet (overleaf). Children should have a copy of the prompt sheet to add their own ticks, or you could enlarge it to A3 poster size and display it in the reading area.

Reading partner prompt sheet

1. Before reading

2. During reading

3. After reading

We think I did ...

Fantastic!   OK   Not so good

Independent reading and the learning environment

Refresh your reading area

Take an objective look at your reading area. Is it comfy and inviting? How are your books organized? How many books are there? What is the balance of old and new books? Tatty favourites are fine and look well-loved, but it's important to have shiny new books too to show that reading and books are valued. As a starting point, consider the following:

- organize your reading area so the books are displayed on open shelves with the front covers facing the child/children,
- limit the number of books to ten fiction and ten non-fiction,
- change your books on a regular basis,
- remember to include comics, magazines and catalogues,
- make sure you provide stories with plenty of action, pace, humour and gadgets for the boys,
- add books that the children have made themselves or that older children have made,
- make the area as comfortable and inviting as possible: provide comfortable seating, floor cushions and settees (full-sized if possible); consider including plants and drapes to add another dimension to the area.

The secret to a successful reading area

Ofsted stated in their *Removing Barriers to Literacy* report in 2011 that the key to the provision of a successful reading area is 'effective and careful monitoring of the area' by staff. For a reading area to really work, there needs to be an adult on hand, showing that they value the space by spending time there: for example, they may be reading by themselves in order to model good practice. Children may want to read to the adult, which is the perfect time to make use of those opportunistic learning moments: reading with expression, talking about the book, and having fun, as well as demonstrating some of the mechanics of reading.

Other reading opportunities around the classroom

Provide children with access to books in areas of the classroom other than the reading area. For example, books about building and transport could be included in a 'construction area'; cookery books could be included in a 'home area' etc.

Make sure there are plenty of opportunities for children to read for a purpose within the indoor and outdoor learning environment. Simple written instructions are a great way of achieving this.

Storytelling spaces, props and play

Where possible, provide storytelling spaces. If you have space in your classroom, consider setting up a separate storytelling area *as well as* a reading area. You could add a storyteller's chair, a hat, lights, and a music player. Remember to add story maps; these act as prompts for the children when role-playing or talking about a story.

Storytelling areas don't need to be indoors. Outdoor storytelling areas are fantastic for all children but particularly boys who love active, outdoor learning.

Tips

If space is at a premium, you could make a 'portable' outdoor storytelling area using a large umbrella that children can sit under. Attach props to the underside of the umbrella (with string, pipe cleaners or Velcro®) that match the features of a story from your reading area, e.g. cut-outs of characters.

The process of reading for pleasure has also been described as a form of play that 'allows us to experience other worlds and roles in our imagination'.[1] Props are a great way of facilitating this playful side of reading.

Audio books

Audio books can be used to stimulate children's imagination and improve listening skills, and are great for modelling reading and hearing different voices. They are particularly effective for EAL children because they will provide children with the means to hear the correct pronunciation of words and to hear the syntactic structure of the language in English.

The Statutory Framework for the Early Years Foundation Stage states that: 'For children whose home language is not English, providers must take reasonable steps to provide opportunities for children to develop and use their home language in play and learning'.[2] Providing audio stories in a child's own language is a great way of fulfilling this statutory requirement.

---

[1] Nell, 1988; cited in Clark and Rumbold, 2006.
[2] Department for Education, *Statutory Framework for the Early Years Foundation Stage*, 2012

Partnership with parents and carers

Parental partnership must be part of a whole-school strategy if it is to be effective in improving outcomes for children. Schools should seek to build a relationship of trust between the school and the home that will lead to effective communication.

Research has identified that the quality of the home learning environment has a massive impact on children's progress.

The Effective Provision of Pre-School Education (EPPE) project identified seven activities that provided clear learning opportunities:

1. reading together
2. going to the library
3. playing with numbers
4. painting and drawing
5. being taught letters
6. being taught numbers
7. songs/poems/rhymes.

Regular participation in these activities can have a significant, positive impact on children's achievement in literacy and numeracy by the age of five.

> *Home Learning Environment (HLE) has the biggest single effect on children's progress, larger than social/economic status (SES), quality of early years education, or any other single factor. Though HLE is associated with SES, the research shows that there are low SES households with good or better HLE and those children make good progress in their learning.*[1]

When parents/carers and practitioners work together, the results have a positive impact on children's development and learning at home and at school. Washbrook and Waldfogel found that children from poorer backgrounds lag behind their more privileged peers in terms of cognitive development; they also found that activities such as reading to children and having fixed bed times can significantly reduce this gap.[2]

[1] Melhuish, E. C., Phan, M. B., Sylva K., Sammons, P., Siraj-Blatchford, I., Taggart, B., 'Effects of the Home Learning Environment and Preschool Center Experience upon Literacy and Numeracy Development in Early Primary School', *Journal of Social Issues* (2008), 64(1): 95–114.

[2] Washbrook, E. and Waldfogel, J., The Sutton Trust *Low income and early cognitive development in the UK*, (2010).

Partnership with parents and carers

Tips

Here are some ways to encourage parents/carers to get involved with their children's reading.

- Share research with parents/carers that shows children who are read to do better in school.
- Invite parents/carers to a meeting about how you teach reading. As part of the event have a professional storyteller tell a story to encourage parents/carers to tell stories about everyday life to their children.
- Invite parents/carers to participate in a phonic or guided reading session in school.
- Encourage parents/carers to involve children in household tasks. Emphasize the importance of naming objects and sequencing the task (explaining what is happening one step at a time).
- Create simple recipe cards or instruction cards for making models. Parents/carers and children can read the cards together as they cook and make models.
- Involve parents/carers in running a book exchange of children's and adult books.
- Encourage parents/carers to read books, newspapers and magazines around the home. Use the slogan 'Read by example'. Ask parents/carers to bring in photographs of themselves reading and display them in the school with appropriate captions.
- Suggest parents/carers provide children with books, comics and writing materials in their bedrooms to encourage children to read and write for pleasure. (On page 30, a door hanger has been provided for children to cut out and colour in.)
- Provide parents/carers with a list of books from a range of authors. Regularly 'spotlight' a book in an area to which parents have access.
- Encourage parents/carers and children to join the local library.

Tips

Here are some suggestions for parents/carers to help their children practise writing letter shapes, words or sentences at home.

- Make a 'writing tray' by spreading rice or couscous onto a tray.
- Provide whiteboards with whiteboard pens.
- Make a personalized writing board by varnishing and decorating a piece of wood – white board pens will wipe off the varnished surface.
- Give their child a washing-up bottle or water pistol filled with water and together write letters or words outside on a hard surface.
- Provide an alphabet frieze to help their child recognize letter shapes.
- Provide opportunities for their child to write for a purpose, for example, birthday cards, shopping lists, to-do lists, lists of toys or games.

Opposite you will find a sheet of simple tips and practical advice for parents/carers on how to support their child with their reading. This can be photocopied or adapted for your own Home-School programme.

TEACHERS
For inspirational support plus free resources and eBooks
www.oxfordprimary.co.uk

PARENTS
Help your child's learning with essential tips, fun activities and free eBooks
www.oxfordowl.co.uk

Reading with your child

Here are some simple tips to help you help your child with reading at home.

Enjoy it!

- Make book sharing a fun time that you both enjoy – snuggle up with a book!
- Read old favourites together as well as new books.
- If your child reads to you, or joins in when you are reading to them, show them that you are proud of what they can do.

Make time and space!

- Make reading a special part of your day. Try to find a time when you aren't busy doing other things so you can spend 'quality time' reading together – even if it's only for a few minutes.
- Try to find a quiet place away from distractions like the television or the computer.
- Try to find some time every day for reading together – 10 minutes each day is better than a long session once a week.

Be positive!

- Give your child lots praise, encouragement and support when they read to you. Focus on what they did well, not what they did wrong. Even small successes are important.
- Never force your child – if they are reluctant to read you could offer a small reward such as playing a game they enjoy. If they are tired or very reluctant, read to them instead.

Find out what they like to read!

- Sometimes we read for pleasure but much of the time we read for a reason. Read lots of different things together – stories, information books, comics, magazines, websites, cereal packets, TV listings – anything you and your child enjoy reading or need to read.
- Let your child make his or her own reading choices sometimes. They need to develop their own personal likes and dislikes. It is OK not to like some books! Don't worry if they choose an 'easy' or favourite book over and over again. This is normal and helps children build their reading confidence and enthusiasm.
- Join the local library and let your child choose from the great range of books on offer.

Talk about it!

FREE parent website to help with your child's learning

www.oxfordowl.co.uk

- Talking about books will help your child become more involved and interested in reading and can help them understand more.
- After you've read a book together – or anything else you choose to read – talk about it. What was it about? How did it make you feel? What did you like or not like about it? What did you learn? Spend some time looking at the pictures and talk about what they tell you. Never cover the pictures while sharing a book.
- You can talk with your child about anything – games, TV programmes, films or other things you do together.

Please knock: Reader inside!

Alien Adventures

© Oxford University Press 2013. Copying permitted within the purchasing school only.

About Project X *Alien Adventures* in Reception/P1

The **Project X *Alien Adventures*** books in Reception/P1 (Book Bands Lilac, Pink, Red and Yellow) provide the perfect support for children taking their very first steps as readers.

From the first wordless books at Lilac Book Band through to Yellow Book Band at the end of Reception/P1, these fully-decodable books offer small steps of phonic progression, coverage of common words (high-frequency, decodable words) and common exception words (high-frequency, tricky words) as well as suffixes and endings (-s, -es, -ing, -er), as outlined in the National Curriculum. This fine levelling ensures that children build stamina and fluency, develop confidence and experience reading success right from day one. For a summary of the phonic, vocabulary and levelling coverage and for a full phonic breakdown of each book, see pages 36–40.

As well as supporting children's decoding skills, **Project X *Alien Adventures*** offers exciting stories, built around the core hooks that all children, but particularly boys, will enjoy: fantastic characters, great plots with plenty of action, gadgets and humour.

In the Sky, Pre-Book Band Lilac A

Cat's Picnic, Book Band Red B

What children say about Project X *Alien Adventures* …

> All my friends like Dr Who so I know they will like this. Billy, age 6

> It's exciting to read about different planets. Lauren, age 7

> It's good because it seems real. Shane, age 6

> It's got scary bits, exciting bits and you don't know what's going to happen in the end so you just have to read it. Daisy, age 7

> It's really, really, really awesome. Joey, age 6

> It's good … really good. Hannah, age 6

The Project X characters

Project X is unique because of its continuous character story. Following the adventures of popular characters is widely acknowledged as one of the best ways to hook young children in to reading … and to keep them reading.[1]

Project X *Alien Adventures* features the characters Max, Cat, Ant and Tiger – four ordinary children who have discovered four amazing watches … watches that allow them to shrink! They have many fantastic and action-packed micro-adventures, exploring an ordinary world made extraordinary by their micro-size.

Max: heroic, kind and generous, the natural leader of the team.

Cat: clever, determined and adventurous.

Ant: intelligent, good at problem-solving, science mad.

Tiger: impetuous, fun-loving, brave.

Meet Nok!

Nok is an alien from Planet Exis who crash-lands on Earth. Although he can shrink and grow like the micro-friends, while on Earth he chooses to stay micro-size to remain safe and stay out of sight. However, Max, Cat, Ant and Tiger find Nok asleep in a log in the park. They soon make friends and start to teach the micro-alien about life on Earth.

Nok is very bright and learns fast, although he sometimes gets things wrong or misunderstands how things work on Earth. He is innocent, enthusiastic and tries to act bravely. His special powers allow him to move or pick things up without touching them and start things (e.g. Tiger's toy trucks or Ant's popcorn maker), but this can sometimes get him into trouble! As a result he brings lots of humour and warmth to the early stories.

The micro-friends' adventures on Earth continue up into Year 1 until one day, while on a school trip to the woods, they find Nok's spaceship under a pile of leaves. They beam on board and meet Seven the robot. Then, Tiger presses a button … and they blast off into space!

An Odd Bug, Book Band Red A

[1] Bookfeast survey 2009 – 51% of children cited character as the main reason for choosing a book.

The Books

Wordless and caption books

The first two **Project X Alien Adventures** books in the Lilac Book Band (Oxford Level 1), *Max's Box* and *In the Sky*, are wordless and support *Letters and Sounds* Phase 1. The next two books, *Splat!* and *Max's Rocket*, use captions and introduce Phase 2, Set 1. All four books are perfect for helping to develop early communication, understanding and comprehension skills.

The rest of the books at Pink, Red and Yellow Book Bands (Oxford Levels 1+–3) follow small steps of phonic progression through Phases 2 and 3 of *Letters and Sounds* as highlighted in the phonics progression chart on pages 36–40.

Splat! Pre-Book Band Lilac B

Features

You will find the following features in the **Project X Alien Adventures** storybooks at Reception/P1 that are designed to stimulate talk and increase engagement:

Spot Nok: early readers can have fun looking for Nok in the artwork in the books (Lilac–Pink Book Bands), helping them to engage with the stories.

Retell the story: story maps appear in all of the Reception/P1 books (Lilac–Yellow Book Bands) and support recall, talk and comprehension activities.

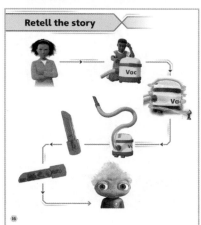

> I really like the 'Retell the story' section ... it's very useful for children after they have read the book.
> Year 1 teacher

About Project X *Alien Adventures* in Reception/P1

33

Project X *Alien Adventures* Companion 1

Inspire a love of reading with this children's companion.

Companion 1 is designed to hook children in to the **Project X** *Alien Adventures* series. It gives more information about the special watches, the characters and the spaceship, as well as comic strip adventures, things to make and do and a poem about Nok's adventures on Earth.

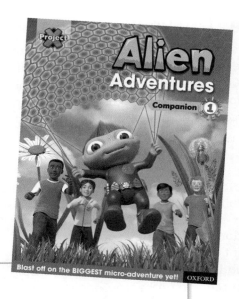

How to use Companion 1

The companion can be used by children working on their own, or it can be shared with a friend/s or an adult. It can be used:

- to introduce the *Alien Adventures* series to the whole class and generate excitement about the individual stories before they read them,
- as a springboard for writing opportunities,
- to help to generate talk with individuals, groups or with the whole class,
- as a perfect solution for wet breaktimes!

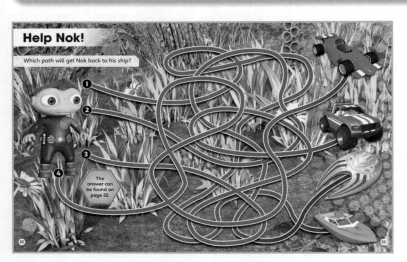

The **Project X** *Alien Adventures* Companion 1 eBook is available free online at www.oxfordprimary.co.uk

Inside Companion 1 you will find …

Story strips: give readers the chance to recap on two key **Project X *Alien Adventures*** stories: how Max, Cat, Ant and Tiger find their special watches, and Nok's crash-landing on Earth. They are perfect for encouraging talk about characters' feelings.

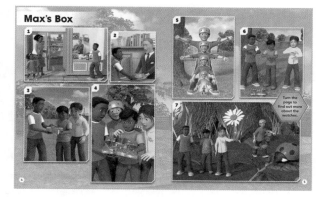

Questions and prompts: provoke thought and provide opportunities for talk, and **'Find out more'** hexagons inspire further reading and encourage children to explore the companion more deeply.

Character profiles: allow readers to get to know the characters in more depth, including their likes and dislikes. You could encourage children to write their own profile.

Gadget and vehicle spreads: give readers more information on the special watches and Nok's spaceship … perfect for inspiring boys.

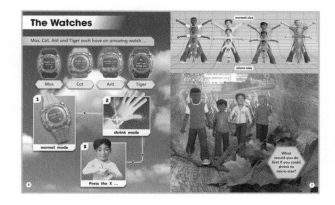

Things to make and do: encourage reading for a purpose and for fun.

Phonic and vocabulary progression for Reception/P1

The chart below shows an overview of the phonic and vocabulary progression for **Project X** *Alien Adventures* until the end of Reception/P1. A full breakdown for each book is provided on subsequent pages.

Oxford Level	Book Band	PX *Alien Adventures* titles	Letters and Sounds phase	Grapheme-Phoneme Correspondences (GPCs) covered	Common words (HFWs: decodable)	Common exception words (HFWs: tricky)	Contractions	Suffixes and endings
1	Lilac A	Max's Box / In the Sky	Phase 1	Wordless books	n/a	n/a	None before Year 1	
1	Lilac B	Splat! / Max's Rocket	Phase 2, Set 1	s, a, t, p	n/a	n/a		
1+	Pink A	The Fishing Trip / Let's Bake!	Phase 2, Set 2	m, i, d, n	in, is, it, dad, and, a	n/a		-s: sits, dips, tips, taps
1+	Pink B	Tin Cat / Sit, Cog Dog!	Phase 2, Set 3	g, o, c, k	on, can, got, not	n/a		
1+	Pink C	Get Ant! / Peg It Up	Phase 2, Set 4	ck, e, u, r	get, up, mum	to, the		
1+	Pink D	Run, Tin Cat! / Peck, Peck	Phase 2, Set 5	h, b, f, l, ff, ll, ss	of, off, back, big	no, go, I		
2	Red A	An Odd Bug / Nok Can Fix It	Phase 3, Set 6	j, v, w, x	will	n/a		-es: presses
2	Red B	Cat's Picnic / A Bag of Tricks	Phase 3, Set 7	y, z, zz, qu	n/a	he, she		
2	Red C	Moths! / Tiger's Fish	Phase 3	ch, sh, th, ng, nk	that, this, then, them, with	we, me, be		-ing: getting, helping
3	Yellow A	On Nok's Trail / I Win!	Phase 3	ai (trail), ee, igh, oa (groans)	see	was		
3	Yellow B	Popcorn Surfing / Stuck in the Mud	Phase 3	oo (look), oo (zooms), ar, or (popcorn), ur	look, too, for	my		
3	Yellow C	The Lost Cow / The Rocket Flight	Phase 3	ow (cow), oi, ear (near), ure, air, er (higher)	down, now	you, they, her, all, are		-er: faster, higher, powers

Phonic and vocabulary progression
Lilac/Pink Book Band (Oxford Levels 1/1+)

Book no.*	Title	Words with known GPCs		Common words (HFWs: decodable)	Common exception words (HFWs: tricky)	Challenge words**
1	Max's Box (Lilac)	Wordless				
2	In the Sky (Lilac)	Wordless				
3	Splat! (Lilac)	s	pat, tap	n/a	n/a	Tiger, Cat, splat
		a				
		t				
		p				
4	Max's Rocket (Lilac)	s	tap(s), pat(s)	n/a	n/a	Max, mum
		a				
		t				
		p				
5	The Fishing Trip (Pink)	i	sits, dips, tin, tips, is, it, in	a, in, is, it, dad	n/a	n/a
		d	dad, sad, dips			
		n	Ant, tin, in			
6	Let's Bake! (Pink)	m	Max, mitt, mad, mmmmmm	in, is, it, dad, and	n/a	Max, Tiger, mitt
		i	tin, mitt, tips, in, it, is			
		d	dad, mad, and			
		n	tin, and			

*Book numbers

Book numbers are given here for teacher reference only, to reflect the small steps of progression throughout the **Project X Alien Adventures** series. The books themselves are not numbered and can be read in any order.

**Challenge words

In these charts, and on the inside cover notes for each book, we've identified the more challenging words children will meet in each story. These 'challenge words' are important for the meaning of the story and most children will be capable of using their decoding and blending skills to read these words. Challenge words include, for example, simple compound words (cobweb, sandpit), simple two-syllable words (rocket, pellet) and words with adjacent consonants (stop, vest, crash). The only truly 'non-decodable' challenge words in these stories are the character names – and only Tiger and Lucy remain non-decodable throughout Phases 2 and 3. However, these names are frequently repeated and quickly become familiar (in the same way as common exception words) so we have included them in the stories.

Phonic and vocabulary progression
Pink Book Band (Oxford Level 1+) cont.

Book no.*	Title	Words with known GPCs		Common words (HFWs: decodable)	Common exception words (HFWs: tricky)	Challenge words**
7	Tin Cat	g	got, sags	on, can, got	n/a	n/a
		o	got, on, nod			
		c	cat, can			
		k	kit			
8	Sit, Cog Dog!	g	Cog Dog, got	got, not	n/a	n/a
		o	Cog Dog, not, got			
		c	Cat, Cog			
		k	kit			
9	Get Ant!	ck	sock, truck, rocket	get, up	the	Max, rocket
		e	rocket, get			
		u	truck, drum, up			
		r	ran, truck, drum, rocket			
10	Peg It Up	ck	socks, pocket, stuck	get, up, mum	to, the	Tiger, Max, pocket, trips, stuck
		e	red, pegs, gets, pocket, end			
		u	sun, mum, up, stuck			
		r	red, trips			
11	Run, Tin Cat!	h	hill	off, back	no, go	bumps, sniff, cross
		b	back, bumps			
		f	fun			
		l	log			
		ff	ruff, off, sniff			
		ll	hill			
		ss	cross, Tess			
12	Peck, Peck	h	hens	of, back, big	I	Max, bucket, pellets, cluck, slips
		b	bucket, big, back			
		f	of			
		l	cluck, slips			
		ff	puff			
		ll	pellets			
		ss	mess			

*/** See page 37 for more details.

Phonic and vocabulary progression
Red Book Band (Oxford Level 2)

Book no.*	Title	Words with known GPCs		Common words (HFWs: decodable)	Common exception words (HFWs: tricky)	Challenge words**
13	An Odd Bug	j	jumps, jok	will	n/a	Tiger, cobweb
		v	vok			
		w	cobweb, wet, twig, will, well			
		x	Max			
14	Nok Can Fix It	v	Vac, vest	will	n/a	button, presses, dust, stuck
		w	will			
		x	Max, fix, X			
15	Cat's Picnic	y	yum, yells, yuck	n/a	she	Cat's, sister, picnic, unzips, presses, twig, stuck
		z	zip, unzips			
		zz	buzz			
		qu	quack, quick			
16	A Bag of Tricks	y	yells, yuck, yes	n/a	he, she	Tiger, Lucy, put, liquid, tricks, presses
		z	zap			
		zz	fizz			
		qu	quick, liquid			
17	Moths!	ch	such	this, then, them, with	we, be	Tiger, fast, helps, spots, crash
		sh	dash, crash			
		th	moth, moths, with, then, them, this			
		ng	wing			
18	Tiger's Fish	ch	much	that, this, then, with	me, be	Tiger, pulls, getting, spots, presses, swims
		sh	ships, fish, shock, shell, shut			
		th	then, with, this, that			
		ng	getting, strong			
		nk	tank			

*/** See page 37 for more details.

Phonic and vocabulary progression
Yellow Book Band (Oxford Level 3)

Book no.*	Title	Words with known GPCs		Common words (HFWs: decodable)	Common exception words (HFWs: tricky)	Challenge words**
19	On Nok's Trail	ai	trail, tail, afraid	see	was	push, sandpit, across, shrink, stack, prints, think
		ee	see, sees, need, creeps			
		igh	might, fright			
		oa	groans			
20	I Win!	ai	trails, wait, sails	see	n/a	bump, Tiger, trucks, boasts, past, shrink
		ee	see, sees, green, speed, stack, prints, think, eek, three			
		igh	high, tight			
		oa	boasts, soaks			
21	Popcorn Surfing	oo	cook, look	look, too, for	my	puts, popcorn, help, munches, shrink
		oo	too, oops			
		ar	starts			
		or	popcorn, corn, for			
		ur	turns, surfs			
22	Stuck in the Mud	oo	look	look	n/a	Tiger, branch, splashes, lightning, push, shrink
		oo	zooms, vroom, pool, oops			
		ar	car, dark, starts, sharp			
		or	storm			
		ur	turns			
23	The Lost Cow	ow	cow, down, now	down, now	you, they, her	asks, Molly, shrinks, faster, grass, puts
		oi	points			
		ear	hears			
		ure	manure			
		air	air			
		er	her, faster			
24	The Rocket Flight	ow	down, how, powers, now	down, now	they, all, are	shrinks, shelf, rocket, flight, fast
		oi	points, avoid			
		ear	near			
		air	air			
		er	higher, powers			

*/** See page 37 for more details.

Observation, assessment and planning

On-going formative assessment is central to good early years practice. By observing what children can do consistently, independently and over time in child-initiated, adult-led and adult-guided learning sessions, practitioners are able to identify where children are in their stage of development. This information can be used for summative assessment. It provides the evidence to support the practitioner to make judgements on whether the child is *emerging*, *expected* or *exceeding* when completing the Early Years Foundation Stage Profile. This information should also be used formatively – to plan next steps in children's learning.

The *Reading assessment record* sheets and *Phonic progression assessment record* sheets on pages 43–47 can be used to record reading skills and behaviours that have been observed in independent reading sessions. They will provide evidence of the stage of development the child has reached in their reading and will support practitioners to make judgements against the Early Years Foundation Stage Profile criteria.

The *Comprehension assessment record* on page 48 will support teachers in assessing the comprehension skills of individual or groups of children at Reception/P1.

Children should be also encouraged to reflect upon their own learning. In the Foundation Stage, adults need to establish a supportive learning climate where children openly talk about their learning. Adults need to model the reflection and questioning process. Engaging children in conversation about their learning and providing oral feedback will help motivate them and build self-esteem. The *Children's 'I can' statements* self-assessment sheets on pages 49–58 can be used as a tool to engage children in reviewing their learning. The 'I can' statements can also be used as learning targets for children to help them with key next steps.

The document *Development Matters in the Early Years Foundation Stage* (Early Education, 2012) provides practitioners with guidance on the observation, assessment and recording process (see overleaf). The developmental statements in the 'Unique child' column will support planning for next steps in children's learning. They identify areas where a child's learning can be challenged and further developed. The guidance in the columns 'Positive relationships' and 'Enabling environments' of the following chart gives examples of what practitioners can do and provide to promote learning. These statements will support the planning process.

Further guidance and assessment support for children exceeding the expectations of the EYFS in reading can be found in the *Project X Alien Adventures Teaching Handbook Year 1/P2*.

Comprehensive support for assessing the full range of children's reading skills and behaviours can be found in the new **Reading Criterion Scale**, developed by Ros Wilson. Go to **www.oxfordprimary.co.uk** for more information.

Development Matters in the Early Years Foundation Stage[1]

Observation, assessment and planning

	Positive relationships (what adults could do):	Enabling environments (what adults could provide):
30–50 months	- Focus on meaningful print such as a child's name, words on a cereal packet or a book title, in order to discuss similarities and differences between symbols. - Help children to understand what a word is by using names and labels and by pointing out words in the environment and in books. - Provide dual language books and read them with all children, to raise awareness of different scripts. Try to match dual language books to languages spoken by families in the setting. - Remember not all languages have written forms and not all families are literate either in English, or in a different home language. - Discuss with children the characters in books being read. - Encourage them to predict outcomes, to think of alternative endings and to compare plots and the feelings of characters with their own experiences. - Plan to include home language and bilingual story sessions by involving qualified bilingual adults, as well as enlisting the help of parents.	- Provide some simple poetry, song, fiction and non-fiction books. - Provide fact and fiction books in all areas, e.g. construction area as well as the book area. - Provide books containing photographs of the children that can be read by adults and that children can begin to 'read' by themselves. - Add child-made books and adult-scribed stories to the book area and use these for sharing stories with others. - Create an environment rich in print where children can learn about words, e.g. using names, signs, posters. - When children can see the text, e.g. using big books, model the language of print, such as *letter, word, page, beginning, end, first, last, middle*. - Introduce children to books and other materials that provide information or instructions. - Carry out activities using instructions, such as reading a recipe to make a cake. - Ensure access to stories for all children by using a range of visual cues and story props.
40–60 months	- Discuss and model ways of finding out information from non-fiction texts. - Provide story sacks and boxes and make them with the children for use in the setting and at home. - Encourage children to recall words they see frequently, such as their own and friends' names. - Model oral blending of sounds to make words in everyday contexts, e.g. 'Can you get your h-a-t hat?' - Play games like word letter bingo to develop children's phoneme-grapheme correspondence. - Model to children how simple words can be segmented into sounds and blended together to make words. - Support and scaffold individual children's reading as opportunities arise.	- Encourage children to add to their first-hand experience of the world through the use of books, other texts and information, and information and communication technology (ICT). - Help children to identify the main events in a story and to enact stories, as the basis for further imaginative play. - Provide storyboards and props which support children to talk about a story's characters and sequence of events. - When children are ready (usually, but not always, by the age of five) provide regular systematic synthetic phonics sessions. These should be multisensory in order to capture their interests, sustain motivation and reinforce learning. - Demonstrate using phonics as the prime approach to decode words while children can see the text, e.g. using big books. - Provide varied texts and encourage children to use all their skills including their phonic knowledge to decode words. - Provide some simple texts which children can decode to give them confidence and to practise their developing skills.

[1] Early Education, *Development Matters in the Early Years Foundation Stage*, © Crown copyright 2012.

Reading assessment record: 30–50 Months

Name of child		✓	Notes
Development Matters: Reading: 30–50 Months[1]	Enjoys rhyming and rhythmic activities		
	Shows awareness of rhyme and alliteration		
	Recognizes rhythm in spoken words		
	Listens to and joins in with stories and poems, one-to-one and also in small groups		
	Joins in with repeated refrains and anticipates key events and phrases in rhymes and stories		
	Beginning to be aware of the way stories are structured		
	Suggests how the story might end		
	Listens to stories with increasing attention and recall		
	Describes main story settings, events and principal characters		
	Shows interest in illustrations and print in books and print in the environment		
	Recognizes familiar words and signs such as own name and advertising logos		
	Looks at books independently		
	Handles books carefully		
	Knows information can be relayed in the form of print		
	Holds books the correct way up and turns pages		
	Knows that print carries meaning		

[1] Early Education, *Development Matters in the Early Years Foundation Stage*. © Crown copyright 2012.

Reading assessment record: 40–60 Months

Name of child	✓	Notes
Continues a rhyming string		
Hears and says the initial sound in words		
Can segment the sounds in simple words and blend them together and knows which letters represent some of them		
Links sounds to letters, naming and sounding the letters of the alphabet		
Begins to read words and simple sentences		
Uses vocabulary and forms of speech that are increasingly influenced by their experiences of books		
Enjoys an increasing range of books		
Knows that information can be retrieved from books and computers		
²**Early learning goal** Children read and understand simple sentences. They use phonic knowledge to decode regular words and read them aloud accurately. They also read some common irregular words. They demonstrate understanding when talking with others about what they have read		

¹Development Matters: Reading: 40–60 Months

¹Early Education, *Development Matters in the Early Years Foundation Stage*, © Crown copyright 2012.
²Department for Education, *Statutory Framework for the Early Years Foundation Stage*, © Crown copyright 2012.

Alien Adventures © Oxford University Press 2013. Copying permitted within the purchasing school only.

Phonic progression assessment record Phase 1

Name of child:

Project X Alien Adventures Book Band Lilac A (Oxford Level 1)

Letters and Sounds[1]			Secure	Not secure	Comments
Phase 1	Aspect 4	Recognises rhyming words			
	Aspect 5	Can identify initial sounds of words			
		Reproduces the initial sounds clearly and recognisably			
		Makes up their own alliterative phrases			
		Can recall the list of objects beginning with the same sound			
		Can offer their own sets of objects and ideas to end the story			
		Can discriminates between the sounds and match to the objects correctly			
		Can discriminate between the sounds and match to the objects correctly			
	Aspect 7	Blends phonemes and recognises the whole word			
		Can say the word and identify the object			
		Blends words that begin with the same initial phoneme			
		Segments words into phonemes			
		Identifies the number of phonemes that make up a given word			

[1]Department for Children, Schools and Families, *Letters and Sounds: Principles and Practice of High Quality Phonics*, © Crown copyright 2007.

© Oxford University Press 2013. Copying permitted within the purchasing school only.

Phonic progression assessment record Phase 2

Name of child:

Project X *Alien Adventures* Book Bands Lilac B to Pink D (Oxford Level 1+)

Letters and Sounds[1]	Grapheme-Phoneme Correspondences (GPCs) covered	Common words (decodable high-frequency words)	Common exception words (tricky words)	Secure	Not secure	Comments
Phase 2, Set 1	s, a, t, p	n/a	n/a			
Phase 2, Set 2	m, i, d, n	a, an, in, is, it, dad, and	n/a			
Phase 2, Set 3	g, o, c, k	on, can, got, not	n/a			
Phase 2, Set 4	ck, e, u, r	get, up, mum	to, the			
Phase 2, Set 5	h, b, f, l, ff, ll, ss	of, off, back, big,	no, go, I,			
Phase 2	Can orally blend and segment CVC words					
	Can find any Phase 2 letter, from a display, when given the sound					

[1] Department for Children, Schools and Families, *Letters and Sounds: Principles and Practice of High Quality Phonics*, © Crown copyright 2007.

© Oxford University Press 2013. Copying permitted within the purchasing school only.

Phonic progression assessment record Phase 3

Name of child:

Project X Alien Adventures Book Bands Red A to Yellow C (Oxford Levels 2 to 3)

Letters and Sounds[1]	Grapheme-Phoneme Correspondences (GPCs) covered	Common words (decodable high-frequency words)	Common exception words (tricky words)	Secure	Not secure	Comments
Phase 3, Set 6	j, v, w, x	will	n/a			
Phase 3, Set 7	y, z, zz, qu	n/a	he, she,			
Phase 3	ch, sh, th, ng, nk	that, this, then, them, with	we, me, be,			
	ai (trail), ee, igh, oa (groans)	see	was			
	oo (look), oo (zooms), ar, or (popcorn), ur	look, too, for	my			
	ow (cow), oi, ear (near), ure, air, er (higher)	down, now	you, they, her, all, are			
	Can give the sound when shown all or most Phase 2 and Phase 3 graphemes					
	Can find all or most Phase 2 and Phase 3 graphemes from a display, when given the sound					
	Can blend and read CVC words (consisting of Phase 2 and 3 graphemes)					
	Can segment and make a phonically plausible attempt at spelling CVC words (consisting of Phase 2 and Phase 3 graphemes)					
	Can write each letter correctly when following a model					

[1]Department for Children, Schools and Families, *Letters and Sounds: Principles and Practice of High Quality Phonics*, © Crown copyright 2007.

Comprehension assessment record: Reception/P1

This chart can be used at any point to assess children's comprehension skills and their developing pleasure in reading and listening to books being read.

Name of child:			
Comprehension Skill	**Secure**	**Not secure**	**Comments**
Can talk about the illustrations in a book.			
Can use the illustrations to gain meaning from a story.			
Can retell an event from a story.			
Can begin to make simple predictions – e.g. how a story might end.			
Can retell a known story in order.			
Can talk about the main point/key events in a story – e.g. characters, setting, main events.			
Can use vocabulary and language that is increasingly influenced by experience of books.			
Can use pictures (unprompted) and words to make meaning.			
With support, can find information to help answer simple, literal questions.			
Can retell stories with growing confidence.			
Is beginning to make predictions about stories based on title, text, blurb or pictures.			
Is developing pleasure in and motivation to read:			
Enjoys looking at and reading books independently.			
Can make simple like/dislike statements about a book.			
Shows curiosity about books.			
Can choose and talk about a book from a selection.			

Alien Adventures © Oxford University Press 2013. Copying permitted within the purchasing school only.

Children's 'I can' statement 1

Linked to the Development Matters *statements for reading*

The practitioner should talk with the child about their learning and then, based on their own observations and the child's responses, complete the sheet together.

I can recognize my name.

I can recognize some other words.

Date:

Observation notes:

Recognizes familiar words and signs such as own name and advertising logos[1]

© Oxford University Press 2013. Copying permitted within the purchasing school only.

[1] Development Matters: 30–50 months. Early Education, *Development Matters in the Early Years Foundation Stage*, © Crown copyright 2012.

Children's 'I can' statement 2

Linked to the Development Matters *statements for reading*

The practitioner should talk with the child about their learning and then, based on their own observations and the child's responses, complete the sheet together.

I can hold a book the right way up.

I can turn the pages.

I know where to start reading.

Date:

Observation notes:

Holds books the correct way up and turns pages

Knows that print carries meaning and, in English, is read from left to right and top to bottom[1]

© Oxford University Press 2013. Copying permitted within the purchasing school only.

[1] Development Matters: 30–50 months. Early Education, *Development Matters in the Early Years Foundation Stage*, © Crown copyright 2012.

Children's 'I can' statement 3

Linked to the Development Matters *statements for reading*

The practitioner should talk with the child about their learning and then, based on their own observations and the child's responses, complete the sheet together.

I can tell my friend what is happening in the story.

I can tell my friend what might happen at the end of the story.

Date:

Observation notes:

Suggests how the story might end

Listens to stories with increasing attention and recall[1]

© Oxford University Press 2013. Copying permitted within the purchasing school only.

[1] Development Matters: 30–50 months. Early Education, *Development Matters in the Early Years Foundation Stage,* © Crown copyright 2012.

Children's 'I can' statement 4

Linked to the Development Matters *statements for reading*

The practitioner should talk with the child about their learning and then, based on their own observations and the child's responses, complete the sheet together.

I can read a book by myself.

Date:

Observation notes:

Looks at books independently[1]

© Oxford University Press 2013. Copying permitted within the purchasing school only.

[1] Development Matters: 30–50 months. Early Education, *Development Matters in the Early Years Foundation Stage,* © Crown copyright 2012.

Children's 'I can' statement 5

Linked to the Development Matters *statements for reading*

The practitioner should talk with the child about their learning and then, based on their own observations and the child's responses, complete the sheet together.

I can say who the characters are in the story.

I can say what the characters were doing in the story.

Date:

Observation notes:

Describes main story settings, events and principal characters[1]

[1] Development Matters: 30–50 months. Early Education, *Development Matters in the Early Years Foundation Stage*, © Crown copyright 2012.

Children's 'I can' statement 6

Linked to the Development Matters *statements for reading*

The practitioner should talk with the child about their learning and then, based on their own observations and the child's responses, complete the sheet together.

I can say words that rhyme.

Date:

Observation notes:

Continues a rhyming string[1]

[1] Development Matters: 40–60 months. Early Education, *Development Matters in the Early Years Foundation Stage*, © Crown copyright 2012.

Children's 'I can' statement 7

Linked to the Development Matters *statements for reading*

The practitioner should talk with the child about their learning and then, based on their own observations and the child's responses, complete the sheet together.

I can say the first sound I hear in a word.

Date:

Observation notes:

Hears and says the initial sound in words[1]

© Oxford University Press 2013. Copying permitted within the purchasing school only.

[1] Development Matters: 40–60 months. Early Education, *Development Matters in the Early Years Foundation Stage*, © Crown copyright 2012.

Children's 'I can' statement 8

Linked to the Development Matters *statements for reading*

The practitioner should talk with the child about their learning and then, based on their own observations and the child's responses, complete the sheet together.

I can blend sounds to read simple words.

Date:

Observation notes:

Can segment the sounds in simple words and blend them together, and knows which letters represent some of them[1]

[1] Development Matters: 40–60 months. Early Education, *Development Matters in the Early Years Foundation Stage,* © Crown copyright 2012.

Children's 'I can' statement 9

Linked to the Development Matters *statements for reading*

The practitioner should talk with the child about their learning and then, based on their own observations and the child's responses, complete the sheet together.

I can read words.

I can read simple sentences.

Date:

Observation notes:

Begins to read words and simple sentences[1]

[1] Development Matters: 40–60 months. Early Education, *Development Matters in the Early Years Foundation Stage*, © Crown copyright 2012.

© Oxford University Press 2013. Copying permitted within the purchasing school only.

Children's 'I can' statement 10

Linked to the Development Matters *statements for reading*

The practitioner should talk with the child about their learning and then, based on their own observations and the child's responses, complete the sheet together.

I can find things in an information book.

I can find information on a computer.

Date:

Observation notes:

Knows that information can be retrieved from books and computers[1]

[1] Development Matters: 40–60 months. Early Education, *Development Matters in the Early Years Foundation Stage,* © Crown copyright 2012.

Alien Adventures

Certificate for FANTASTIC reading

has been awarded this certificate for

Alien Adventures

Certificate for FANTASTIC writing

has been awarded this certificate for

© Oxford University Press 2013. Copying permitted within the purchasing school only.

Project X *Alien Adventures* and the Scottish Curriculum for Excellence

The **Project X *Alien Adventures*** series has been rigorously developed to reflect and support the principles and practice of the Scottish CfE. There is a direct correlation between the advice on teaching literacy developed in **Project X *Alien Adventures*** and in recent guidance from CfE. In particular, the following issues are currently highlighted in Scottish education:

Personalization and choice

The Scottish CfE encourages teachers to make professional decisions about the choice and use of teaching resources in their classrooms. **Project X *Alien Adventures*** is designed to be used flexibly, depending on the needs of pupils, and is an exciting addition to the early years literacy tool kit. Suggestions for innovative ways of using the resource are outlined on pages 10–13.

The Scottish CfE stresses the importance of developing the ability to learn independently, encouraging children to set their own personal reading targets and take responsibility for their own learning. As part of the **Project X *Alien Adventures*** resource, there are free films online, demonstrating best practice in how to develop independent readers in early years. For more information visit: **www.oxfordprimary.co.uk**.

The Scottish CfE recommends choice for pupils in the selection of reading books; the **Project X *Alien Adventures*** gives children the opportunity to practise reading phonically-regular and high-frequency words that have been learned previously, using core reading schemes. Young readers already familiar with sight vocabulary and with an understanding of how to use their phonic skills to decode words will enjoy choosing a book from an appropriately colour-coded group of publications. The Scottish CfE emphasizes the dynamic sense of power that children experience when they first read a new book without the help of an adult. It is at this turning point in their development that they know and believe that they are 'readers'.

Reading engagement

The Scottish CfE recognizes the findings of research, indicating that there is a link between reading success, the enjoyment of books and the number of books that children read. 'Enjoyment', 'motivation', 'exploration' and 'challenge' is key vocabulary in the learning outcomes for reading in the CfE. In Scotland, there is concern about how to close the gap in attainment between girls and boys, caused by this lack of engagement in reading and writing among boys. **Project X *Alien Adventures*** books appeal to boys with their colourful, digitally enhanced pictures, modern themes and exciting stories. Girls and boys connect with the upbeat characters and enjoy the challenge of reading new books and the pleasure of returning, by choice, to the familiarity of old favourites.

The connection between watching stories unfold on screen and reading stories is emphasized through the motivating **Project X** *Alien Adventures* animations, available free, online at: www.oxfordprimary.co.uk. The Scottish CfE emphasizes the development of confident, successful young people and the celebration of effort and success is a feature of school life in Scotland. The certificates (see pages 59–60), bookmarks and other free downloadables accompanying **Project X** *Alien Adventures* will be a welcome addition to school assemblies (for more details visit www.oxfordprimary.co.uk).

Young readers who crave detail about the characters, places and gadgets which they read about will find all this in the motivating companion books that accompany the series (see pages 34–35). All children will engage with *Alien Adventures*, but particularly those who already know the four main characters through the **Project X** guided/group reading books (see pages 4–5 for more details or visit www.oxfordprimary.co.uk).

Partnerships with parents

Educating parents about the importance of supporting their children's developing literacy is a priority in Scotland. Early years educators and teachers will welcome the practical methods suggested in this handbook to encourage parental involvement (see pages 27–30). Also, the clear step-by- step guidance on the inside covers of the children's books, on how to support children's reading, is invaluable for parents. Interesting follow-up activities to teach comprehension are also suggested on inside covers. This advice will enhance the learning experience at home with parent and child and reflects exactly the same advice as that being offered by the Scottish Book Trust and various local authority and government initiatives in Scotland.

TEACHERS
For inspirational support plus free resources and eBooks
www.oxfordprimary.co.uk

PARENTS
Help your child's learning with essential tips, fun activities and free eBooks
www.oxfordowl.co.uk

Transitions, active learning and learning through play

Recent CfE guidance focuses on the difficulties that primary pupils experience at the point of transfer from stage to stage in school but particularly in the transition from nursery to primary school. A reading resource such as **Project X** *Alien Adventures* helps to bridge different areas and brings coherence to the area of reading. Children welcome well-known characters as they progress from Lilac, wordless books to the early phonics Pink books and on to more complex Red and Yellow levels. Approaches to learning recommended in this handbook ensure consistency of experience from nursery to P1.

Building on excellent nursery practice and ensuring that transition is as seamless as possible, P1 teachers in Scotland are encouraged to adopt early years' approaches to learning, with an emphasis on structured play and active learning developed through collaborative and co-operative group work. These are the approaches to early reading recommended in this handbook (see pages 19–24). Downloadable games also encourage active learning.

Synthetic phonics, word recognition and comprehension

The impact of a rigorous phonics programme on a child's ability to read has long been recognized and encouraged in Scotland. These programmes follow a similar progression in the introduction of sounds as **Project X Alien Adventures**. Phonics programmes run alongside the teaching of non-decodable high-frequency words, derived from the Dolche list of 100 most used words in children's writing. With a few exceptions, these words are the same as vocabulary used in **Project X Alien Adventures**. In these crucial aspects, this resource articulates very well with Scotland's CfE.

> For a summary of the phonic and levelling coverage and for a full phonic breakdown of each book, see pages 36–40.

In the area of comprehension, the Scottish CfE encourages group discussion of ideas, with children generating their own questions and observations about texts. As with advice on approaches to reading in **Project X Alien Adventures**, pupils are encouraged to link ideas in reading to their own experience and then to reflect upon and interpret ideas in the text through drama, art and writing, sometimes individually and sometimes in groups.

The active learning recommended by the Scottish CfE includes paired reading and various models of reading partnerships. This handbook features practical advice on setting up reading partnerships, alongside ideas for how to train partners and useful resources such as a 'prompt' sheet (see pages 23–24).

Assessment

Formative assessment underpins all learning in classrooms in Scotland and includes peer- and self-assessment for children's learning. Approaches to reading assessment in **Project X Alien Adventures** fit well with best practice, particularly with the emphasis on children being involved in the assessment of their own learning (see pages 41–58 for more information).

Project X Alien Adventures can help teachers in delivering the experiences and outcomes in Reading, and Listening and Talking as listed on the following page. It also provides a range of follow-up activities to support children's writing.

Curriculum for Excellence Literacy and English experiences and outcomes

Year	Oxford Level	Book Band		Project X *Alien Adventures* books	Objectives
Primary 1	1	Pre-Book Bands Lilac	A	• Max's Box • In the Sky	**Listening and Talking/Reading** • I enjoy exploring and choosing stories and other texts to watch, read or listen to, and can share my likes and dislikes. LIT 0–01b/LIT 0–11b • To help me understand stories and other texts, I ask questions and link what I am learning with what I already know. LIT 0–7a/LIT 0–16a/ENG 0–17a • I enjoy exploring events and characters in stories and other texts, sharing my thoughts in different ways. LIT 0–19a
			B	• Splat! • Max's Rocket	**Listening and Talking** • I listen or watch for useful or interesting information and I use this to make choices or learn new things. LIT 0–04a • As I listen and take part in conversations and discussions, I discover words and phrases which I use to help me express my ideas, thoughts and feelings. LIT 0–10a **Listening and Talking/Reading** • I enjoy exploring and playing with the patterns and sounds of language and can use what I learn. LIT 0–01a/LIT 0–11a/LIT 0–20a • I enjoy exploring and choosing stories and other texts to watch, read or listen to, and can share my likes and dislikes. LIT 0–01b/LIT 0–11b • I explore sounds, letters and words discovering how they work together, and I can use what I learn to help me as I read and write. ENG 0–12a/LIT 0–13a/LIT 0–21a • To help me understand stories and other texts, I ask questions and link what I am learning with what I already know. LIT 0–7a/LIT 0–16a/ENG 0–17a • I enjoy exploring events and characters in stories and other texts, sharing my thoughts in different ways. LIT 0–19a **Listening and Talking/Writing** • I enjoy exploring events and characters in stories and other texts and I use what I learn to invent my own, sharing these with others in imaginative ways. LIT 0–09b/LIT 0–31a
	1+	1 Pink	A	• The Fishing Trip • Let's Bake!	
			B	• Tin Cat • Sit, Cog Dog!	
			C	• Get Ant! • Peg It Up	
			D	• Run, Tin Cat! • Peck, Peck	
	2	2 Red	A	• An Odd Bug • Nok Can Fix It	
			B	• Cat's Picnic • A Bag of Tricks	
			C	• Moths! • Tiger's Fish	
	3	3 Yellow	A	• On Nok's Trail • I Win!	
			B	• Popcorn Surfing • Stuck in the Mud	
			C	• The Lost Cow • The Rocket Flight	

Project X *Alien Adventures* and the Foundation Phase in Wales

The **Project X *Alien Adventures*** series has been developed in line with the National Literacy and Numeracy Framework (2013) and the Foundation Phase Framework for Children's Learning for 3- to 7-year-olds in Wales (2008). The Framework ensures that, through their experiences in the seven Areas of Learning, children should grow, develop and progress in their development.

In particular, **Project X *Alien Adventures*** aims to support teachers in delivering the Language, Literacy and Communication Skills area, Oracy and Reading strands.

Language, Literacy and Communication Skills

Children in the Foundation Phase should be encouraged to listen and respond to others. They should have opportunities to choose and use reading materials and understand the conventions of print and books. The Foundation Phase curriculum framework requires structured opportunities to develop literacy skills; encouraging the use of **Project X *Alien Adventures*** for independent reading can help to fulfill this statutory requirement.

Oracy

Speaking, listening and viewing activities in the Foundation Phase should enable children to make progress in their ability to listen and respond appropriately and effectively, with growing attention and concentration. The **Project X *Alien Adventures*** animations and the companion books are perfect for introducing the series in a class session; they can help provoke discussion, build anticipation and generate a 'buzz' around reading independently. For more information on the companions, see pages 34–35, and to watch the animations, visit: **www.oxfordprimary.co.uk**.

Skills

Children should be given opportunities to experience a range of stimuli. The **Project X *Alien Adventures*** series provides support for teachers in developing oracy; as well as the animations and companion books mentioned above, the questions provided on the inside cover notes of each of the books offer plenty of discussion points for adults to use with the children, before and after reading. Furthermore, each book in the Foundation Phase concludes with an opportunity to retell the story in sequence using a range of vocabulary.

> For more information on the importance of encouraging talk and how **Project X *Alien Adventures*** supports speaking and listening, see pages 10–11, 15 and 21–24.

Range

The Foundation Phase curriculum encourages a balance of teacher-led and child-initiated opportunities for oracy. **Project X Alien Adventures** would cover the following range points: retelling stories, both real and imagined; talking of matters of immediate and personal interest; and expressing thoughts, ideas and feelings. It would also include expressing opinions, predicting outcomes and discussing possibilities. The stories will encourage children to participate in role-play and drama activities as they follow the adventures of the micro-friends.

Reading

The **Project X Alien Adventures** series offers a wide range of exciting fiction books to engage children. The stories introduce readers to the core characters, Max, Cat, Ant, Tiger and their new alien friend, Nok. Readers follow these characters as they pursue many exciting micro-adventures, face challenges and make choices (see pages 31–32 for more information about their adventures in the Foundation Phase). There is a particular focus on engaging boys at the beginning of their reading journey in order to encourage a lifelong love of reading (for more information on boys' reading, see pages 14–16).

Skills

The Foundation Phase curriculum requires that children should enjoy reading and make progress in their ability to show an interest in books, enjoy their content and handle them as a reader. The **Project X Alien Adventures** are lively, engaging stories, designed to stimulate the interest and enjoyment of early readers.

In the Foundation Phase curriculum it states that children need to understand that written symbols have sound and meaning. They need to be helped to develop their phonological, graphic and grammatical knowledge, together with word recognition and contextual understanding. This should be within a balanced and coherent programme. **Project X Alien Adventures** has a **structured phonics progression** which fully supports this approach. The small steps of fine levelling mean that children gradually develop the self-assurance to tackle more challenging texts. As their confidence grows, they will also increase their fluency, accuracy, understanding and independence.

> For a summary of the phonic and levelling coverage and for a full phonic breakdown of each book, see pages 36–40.

In addition, children should be encouraged to read texts aloud and respond to them; they should be able to talk about characters, events, language and information as they predict events and explore meaning. The questions on the inside cover notes of the **Project X Alien Adventures** books and the follow-up activities on the Photocopiable Masters in this handbook support this development of emerging comprehension skills.

Range

The Foundation Phase curriculum encourages a balance of teacher-led and child-initiated opportunities for reading. **Project X Alien Adventures** would cover the following range points: children should be given opportunities to read individually including picture books and stories based on imaginary or fantasy worlds.

The **Project X** *Alien Adventures* books are presented in a 3D digital illustration style. A number of them are available in eBook form, which gives children the opportunity to use computer-based materials.

TEACHERS
For inspirational support plus free resources and eBooks
www.**oxford**primary.co.uk

PARENTS
Help your child's learning with essential tips, fun activities and free eBooks
www.**oxford**owl.co.uk

Language, Literacy and Communication Skills outcomes

Children's progress through **Project X** *Alien Adventures* books will vary. This would be reflected in the level achieved in their Foundation Phase Outcome for Language, Literacy and Communication skills.

- Lilac band would be within Outcome 3.
- Pink, Red and Yellow bands would be within Outcomes 4–6.

(See pages 46–47 of *Framework for Children's Learning for 3 to 7-year-olds in Wales*, 2008)

Assessment

Progress of children in the Foundation Phase in Wales is assessed using The Foundation Phase Child Assessment Profile (2011) (current at time of writing). Descriptions of Behaviour are grouped into six Developmental Areas. Each area is monitored following a baseline assessment on entry to formal education. The method of assessment is subject to change; however, use of **Project X** *Alien Adventures* would enhance skills in the **Speaking and Listening** and **Reading and Writing** developmental areas.

Speaking and Listening

- **4a** Asks a variety of questions.
- **7b** Shows an understanding of the main points of a story or information given.

Reading and Writing

- **3b** Shows awareness of differences between 'reading' print and following pictures in stories.
- **4b** Recognizes that letters make sounds that go together to make words.
- **5a** Recognizes familiar and high-frequency words by sight in simple text.
- **6a** Expresses opinions about what has been read.
- **6c** Reads simple text.

Project X *Alien Adventures* and the Northern Ireland Curriculum

Project X *Alien Adventures* supports the aims and objectives of the Northern Ireland Curriculum for Literacy and Language in the Foundation Stage.

Encouraging a disposition to read

Project X *Alien Adventures* features engaging 3D digital illustrations which children love, exciting character-based stories, and first wordless books at Lilac book band, all of which can help you to provide a rich literacy environment where children can choose appropriate stories, experience books independently and foster a disposition towards reading from the earliest stage.

Independent reading

Alongside modelled, shared and guided reading undertaken in the Foundation Stage, **Project X *Alien Adventures*** provides the perfect support for children taking their very first steps as independent readers. The first books at Lilac book band are wordless stories, which enable children to develop early communication, understanding and comprehension skills as well as simply choosing and experiencing books independently.

From Pink Book Band, the fully decodable books begin to offer small steps of phonic progression. However, if a child can't decode the text at these early stages, it doesn't matter. It's just as important for them to experience enjoying the stories and talking about the pictures. For a summary of the phonic and levelling coverage and for a full phonic breakdown of each book, see pages 36–40.

> For information on how to use **Project X *Alien Adventures*** to support modelled reading, see pages 19–20.

The importance of talking and listening

The importance of talk and other forms of communication in developing children's literacy and wider social skills is widely recognized. The **Project X *Alien Adventures*** books have been designed to stimulate talk and there is support within the books for exploring characters, retelling stories, raising and responding to questions, and expressing opinions.

> For more information on how **Project X *Alien Adventures*** supports talking and listening, see pages 21–24.

Using ICT

Project X *Alien Adventures* supports the creative use of ICT, emphasized in the Northern Ireland Curriculum. All of the stories feature an engaging, detailed, 3D digital illustration style. A number of **Project X** *Alien Adventures* eBooks can be accessed free online to support the development of multimedia literacy skills. The **Project X** *Alien Adventures* animations and the companion books can be used to generate excitement about the series in a class session. To watch the animations, visit: **www.oxfordprimary.co.uk**, and for more information on the companions, see pages 34–35.

Assessment

The continuous cycle of on-going assessment, outlined in the Northern Ireland Curriculum, is supported in the form of teacher assessment record sheets to help teachers observe children's progress (see pages 41–48). There are also simple self-assessment sheets to support young learners in thinking about their learning (see pages 49–58).

Thinking, problem solving and decision making

The **Project X** *Alien Adventures* stories present readers with a range of scenarios in which our core characters are faced with problems, challenges and decisions to make. By following the adventures of Max, Cat, Ant, Tiger and Nok, readers can learn to empathize with situations and explore their own problem-solving skills.

Statutory Requirements for Language and Literacy in the Foundation Stage

Project X *Alien Adventures* can help you deliver the following statutory requirements for *Talking and listening* and *Reading*. Inside cover notes and Photocopiable Masters for each book provide a range of discussion points and follow-up activities, including ideas for writing activities.

Talking and listening

Pupils should be enabled to develop:

- attention and listening skills through:
  - listening to a wide range of stories, poems, songs and music;
  - following instructions;
  - recalling sequence and detail.
- phonological awareness through:
  - identifying words in phrases and sentences;
  - identifying syllables;
  - identifying and manipulating phonemes.
- social use of language through:
  - observing modelled behaviours;
  - talking with adults and other pupils;
  - initiating and joining in conversations in pairs or groups;
  - adopting or assuming a role relevant to context.
- language and thinking through:
  - talking about experiences, pictures and stories;
  - naming;
  - recalling;
  - sequencing;
  - predicting;
  - asking and answering questions;
  - describing;
  - explaining;
  - sharing their thoughts, feelings and ideas with different audiences.
- an extended vocabulary through:
  - listening and responding to adults and peers;
  - an immersion in the language of books, both fiction and non-fiction.

Progression

As pupils progress through the Foundation Stage they should be enabled to:

- express themselves with increasing clarity and confidence, using a growing vocabulary and more complex sentence structure;
- understand and use social conventions in conversations and pupil initiated interactions;
- initiate and sustain conversations with adults and peers in the classroom;
- retell stories, events or personal experiences in sequence with reasonable detail;
- answer questions to give information and demonstrate understanding;
- ask questions to find information or seek an explanation;
- offer reasons to support opinions given;
- listen with increasing attentiveness and for longer periods of time;
- listen to and carry out increasingly complex instructions.

Reading

Through modelled, shared and guided reading sessions pupils should be enabled to:

- read with some independence;
- read a range of texts including electronic texts and those composed by themselves and others;
- sequence stories in reasonable detail using appropriate language;
- use word structure to develop reading;
- develop auditory discrimination and memory;
- develop visual discrimination and memory;
- share a range of books with adults/other pupils;
- know how to handle and care for books;
- understand and use some language associated with books;
- select and use books for specific purposes;
- develop concepts of print;
- listen to a range of stories, poems and non-fiction texts read to them by adults/other pupils.

Progression

As pupils progress through the Foundation Stage they should be enabled to:

- understand that words are made up of sounds and syllables and that sounds are represented by letters (phoneme/grapheme awareness);
- recognize different types of text and identify specific features of some genres;
- read and follow simple instructions;
- use a range of reading cues with increasing independence and begin to self-correct;
- read on sight some words in a range of meaningful contexts;
- begin to read with expression in response to print variations and punctuation;
- use extended vocabulary when discussing text, retelling stories or in their emergent writing;
- make links between personal experience and the text;
- make and give reasons for predictions;
- understand the purpose of and use environmental print;
- browse and choose books for a specific purpose.

Photocopiable Masters

Book Bands Lilac to Yellow
(Oxford Levels 1 to 3)

1 Name _____ Date _____

Whose watch is it?

Colour in the watches. Then draw a line from the character to their watch.

Pre-Book Band Lilac A (Oxford Level I) • Max's Box

Sequencing *In the Sky*

Cut out the pictures. Then put them in the right order to tell the story.

What starts with 's'

Look at the picture and write the letter 's' next to all the things that begin with the sound /s/.

Pre-Book Band Lilac B (Oxford Level 1) ● Splat!
© Oxford University Press 2013. Copying permitted within the purchasing school only.

Taps!

Write the word 'taps' in the blank spaces. In which sentence does the word mean something different?

The rain __ __ __ __ .

Max __ __ __ __ Mum.

Turn on the __ __ __ __ .

Pre-Book Band Lilac B (Oxford Level 1) • Max's Rocket

5 Name _____ Date _____

Match the fish

Draw a line from each baby fish to its mother that has the same letter. Say the sound of the letter when you join them up.

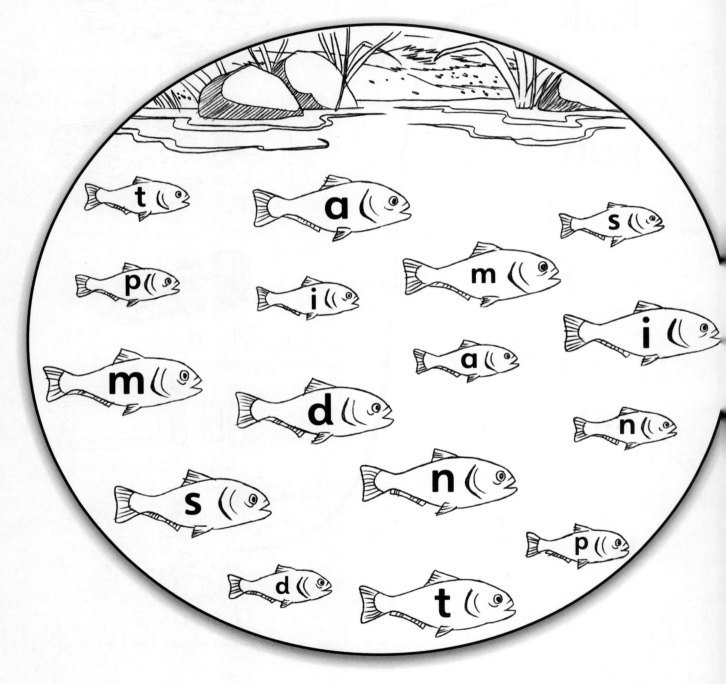

Book Band Pink A (Oxford Level 1+) • **The Fishing Trip**

6 Name _____ Date _____

Match the word

Match the word to the picture.

Nok	
pan	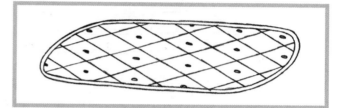
mat	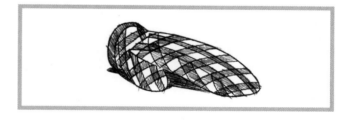
tin	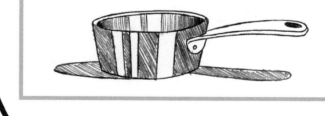
tap	
mitt	

Pre-Book Band Pink A (Oxford Level 1+) ● Let's Bake!
© Oxford University Press 2013. Copying permitted within the purchasing school only.

What can Tin Cat do?

Draw a line from the word to the picture that shows what Tin Cat can do.

nod   sit

nap   sag

Book Band Pink B (Oxford Level 1+) • Tin Cat

8 Name _____ Date _____

Make a sentence

Colour in the picture of Cog Dog.
Cut out the words and put them into
a sentence underneath the picture.

did	sit.	Dog
not		Cog

Book Band Pink B (Oxford Level 1+) • Sit, Cog Dog!
© Oxford University Press 2013. Copying permitted within the purchasing school only.

q Name _____ Date _____

Where did Max look?

Read each word. Draw a circle around the places where Max looked for Ant.

rock

sock   rocket

mat   step

drum   truck   top

Book Band Pink C (Oxford Level 1+) • Get Ant!
© Oxford University Press 2013. Copying permitted within the purchasing school only.

| 10 | Name _____ Date _____ |

The missing word

Look at the picture and read the sentence.
Write the missing word in the sentence.

Tiger is stuck in the _____ .

peg   sock   pocket   sun

Book Band Pink C (Oxford Level 1+) • Peg It Up
© Oxford University Press 2013. Copying permitted within the purchasing school only.

11 Name _____ Date _____

Sequencing sentences

Cut out the sentences. Then read the sentences and put them in the correct order.

Tin Cat runs up the hill.

A man gets the cross dog.

Ant gets up on Tin Cat.

Ant and Tin Cat go in the log.

Tin Cat runs away.

Tin Cat bumps into a dog.

Book Band Pink D (Oxford Level 1+) • **Run, Tin Cat!**

12 Name _____ Date _____

Making words

Draw lines between the sets of letters to make the words you have read in the story.

clu   ps

pu   ss

me   ck

pe   ff

sli   ck

Fill in the missing words.

The hens __ __ __ __ .

Ant is a __ __ __ __ .

Book Band Pink D (Oxford Level 1+) • Peck, Peck

13 Name _____ Date _____

Rhyming words

How many words can you think of that rhyme with 'log'? Write them in a list below.

log

Book Band Red A (Oxford Level 2) ● **An Odd Bug**

Sequencing *Nok Can Fix It*

Cut out the pictures. Then put them in the right order.

15 Name _____ Date _____

Picnic puzzle

Draw a line to the word that completes the sentence.

Nok is stuck in the	box.
Cat unzips the	Nok.
The duck picks up	mud.
Nok is in the	bag.

Book Band Red B (Oxford Level 2) • Cat's Picnic

Picture matching

Match the sentences to the pictures.

Lucy tricks Tiger.

Lucy has a sip.

Lucy tricks Cat.

Lucy tricks Max.

Lucy jumps.

Tiger's thought bubble

What might Tiger be thinking?
Write it in the bubble.

Book Band Red C (Oxford Level 2) • Moths!

Snap pictures

Cut out the pictures. Use them to play snap or pairs.

Book Band Red C (Oxford Level 2) • Tiger's Fish

Missing letters

Read the sentences. Use the letters on the footprints to help fill in the blanks.

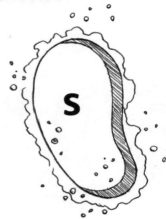

Ant thinks Nok might ___ee___ help.

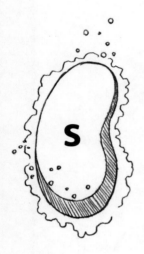

Max ___ee___ a long tail.

The cat ___ ___ee___ ___ up on Nok.

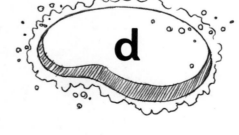
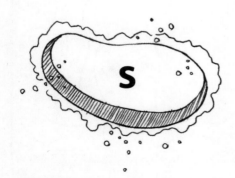

Book Band Yellow A (Oxford Level 3) • On Nok's Trail

Write all about it!

What is happening in each picture?
Write a sentence to match.

Book Band Yellow A (Oxford Level 3) • I Win!

| 21 | Name _____ Date _____ |

Popcorn words

Use the letters to make as many words as you can from the story. You can use each letter more than once. Write them in a list below.

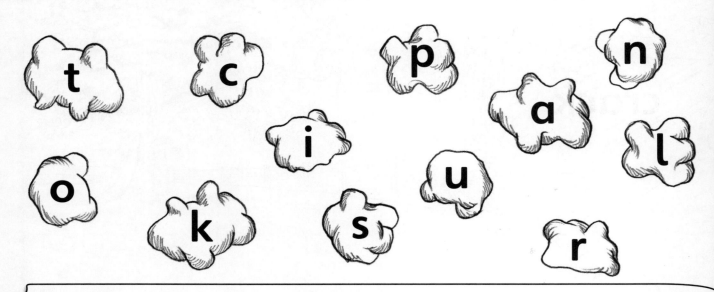

Book Band Yellow B (Oxford Level 3) • Popcorn Surfing

Noisy words

Can you say the noisy word and draw a picture from the book to match each one?

crack

vroom!

zap!

Book Band Yellow B (Oxford Level 3) • **Stuck in the Mud**

23 Name _____ Date _____

Farm animals

Match the picture of the animal to its name. Then colour in the animals.

sheep

cow

goat

hen

duck

Book Band Yellow C (Oxford Level 3) • The Lost Cow
© Oxford University Press 2013. Copying permitted within the purchasing school only.

Moving words

Can you say the word and draw a picture from the book to match each one?

up

down

spin

Book Band Yellow C (Oxford Level 3) ● **The Rocket Flight**

25

Name _____ Date _____

Max

Think about what you know about Max. Colour him in and then write down words to complete the sentences.

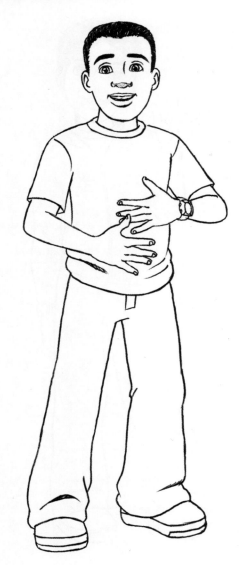

He is _____

He has _____

Alien Adventures © Oxford University Press 2013. Copying permitted within the purchasing school only.

Cat

Think about what you know about Cat. Colour her in and then write down words to complete the sentences.

She is _____

She has _____

27 Name _____ Date _____

Ant

Think about what you know about Ant. Colour him in and then write down words to complete the sentences.

He is _____

He has _____

28 Name _____ Date _____

Tiger

Think about what you know about Tiger. Colour him in and then write down words to complete the sentences.

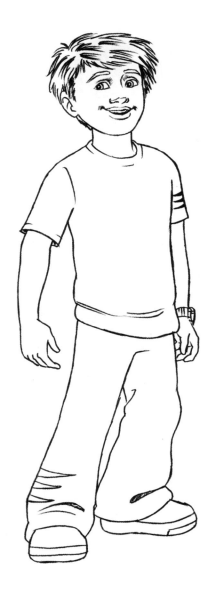

He is _____

He has _____

29

Name _____ Date _____

Nok

Think about what you know about Nok. Colour him in and then write down words to complete the sentences.

He is _____

He has _____

Alien Adventures © Oxford University Press 2013. Copying permitted within the purchasing school only.

30 Name _____ Date _____

My shrinking watch

Design a shrinking watch.

My design

What my watch does:

My watch can make me shrink.

My watch _____

_____

_____

_____

31 Name _____ Date _____

My character

Draw a picture of your new character then write about them. What are they called? Where do they come from? What do they like doing?

My story character

_____

_____

_____

Story mountain

Use the mountain below to help you to plan your story.

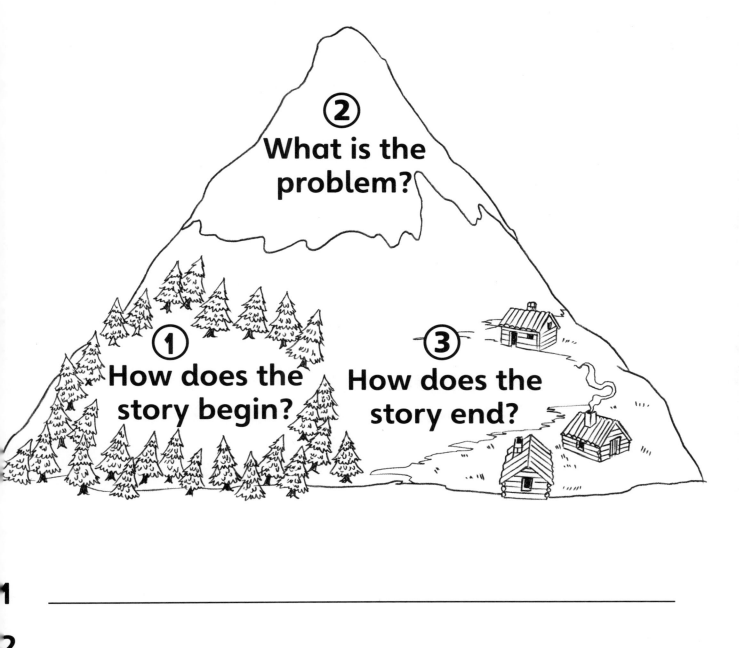

1 _____

2 _____

3 _____

33 Name _____ Date _____

I can sequence a story

Tell the story to a friend. Then in the boxes, draw a picture or write a sentence to say what happened. Use what you have drawn or written to tell the story again.

First

Then

Finally